GREAT WAR LITERATURE

A-LEVEL NOTES

Written by W Lawrance

on

JOURNEY'S END

A PLAY BY R. C. SHERRIFF

Great War Literature A-Level Notes on Journey's End a Play by R C Sherriff
Written by W Lawrance

Published by:
Great War Literature Publishing LLP
Forum House, Stirling Road, Chichester PO19 7DN
Web site: www.greatwarliterature.co.uk
E-Mail: enquiries@greatwarliterature.co.uk

Produced in Great Britain

First Published October 2006. Copyright © Wendy Lawrance 2006 - 2013
The moral right of the author has been asserted.

ISBN 978-1905378289 (1905378289) Paperback Edition 2
Replaces earlier edition: 9781905378401

Design and production by Great War Literature Publishing LLP
Typeset in Neue Helvetica, ITC Berkeley Old Style and Trajan Pro

Great War Literature A-Level Notes on

Journey's End
a play by R. C. Sherriff

CONTENTS

Preface

The primary purpose of Great War Literature Notes is to provide in-depth analysis of First World War literature for A-Level students.

Great War Literature Publishing have taken the positive decision to produce a more detailed and in-depth interpretation of selected works for students. We also actively promote the publication of our works in an electronic format via the Internet to give the broadest possible access.

Our publications can be used in isolation or in collaboration with other study guides. It is our aim to provide assistance with your understanding of First World War literature, not to provide the answers to specific questions. This approach provides the resources that allow the student the freedom to reach their own conclusions and express an independent viewpoint.

Great War Literature Study Guides can include elements such as biographical detail, historical significance, character assessment, synopsis of text, and analysis of poetry and themes.

The structure of Great War Literature Study Guides allows the reader to delve into a required section easily without the need to read from beginning to end. This is especially true of our e-Books.

The Great War Literature Study Guides have been thoroughly researched and are the result of over 30 years of experience of studying this particular genre.

Students must remember that studying literature is not about being right or wrong, it is entirely a matter of opinion. The secret to success is developing the ability to form these opinions and to deliver them succinctly and reinforce them with quotes and clear references from the text.

Great War Literature Study Guides help to extend your knowledge of First World War literature and offer clear definitions and guidance to enhance your studying. Our clear and simple layouts make the guides easy to access and understand.

This new edition of the Great War Literature A-Level Study Guide on *Journey's End*, while based on our GCSE guide, provides several new chapters and more detail and has been produced in response to requests and suggestions received from schools and examining boards, giving you the most valuable resource available.

INTRODUCTION

This play was originally performed in December 1928 and published the following year. The action takes place in a dugout, in a British trench near St Quentin in France. This is a story of the relationships between five officers between 18th and 21st March 1918, immediately prior to a major battle.

We experience everything from mundane discussions regarding the merits of pineapple over apricots, to the death of one of the officers and the impact this has on those left behind.

There are many moments of humour in the play, particularly at the beginning, which serve to intensify the horrors which the men are experiencing. By introducing humour and detailed personalities into the play, Sherriff demonstrates the human cost of the war which destroyed a generation of young men, the like of which would never be seen again.

JOURNEY'S END
A PLAY BY R. C. SHERRIFF

SYNOPSIS

ACT ONE

The play opens with Captain Hardy, alone in the dugout, trying to dry his sock, while singing a song to himself. Osborne arrives and the two men share a drink while Hardy finishes dressing. Hardy's regiment is being replaced at the front by Osborne's and the two men discuss what has been happening lately, and the likelihood of a German attack. They talk about the layout and condition of the dugout and trenches and Hardy hands over a list of supplies. The conversation turns to Stanhope - Osborne's company commander. Hardy appears critical of Stanhope's drinking, but Osborne defends him. Although Hardy should really wait and hand over to Stanhope personally, he chooses not to and leaves Osborne to pass on his messages.

The officers' servant - a soldier named Mason - appears and he and Osborne discuss that night's meal. Raleigh arrives: he is a new officer, fresh from England. Osborne welcomes him and, over a drink, it soon becomes clear that Raleigh already knows Stanhope. He explains that they had been at the same school, although Stanhope is three years older. Raleigh's devotion to his old school friend is obvious - in fact it would seem that Raleigh has used some of his family's influence to ensure that he would be assigned to Stanhope's Company. He reveals that Stanhope and his sister share a close friendship, a fact of which Osborne had not previously been aware. Osborne seems concerned that Raleigh might notice some changes in Stanhope and tries to prepare him, as well as explaining some of the routine of the dugout and the trenches.

Raleigh is introduced to Mason, who is worried because a tin which he thought contained pineapple chunks, turns out to be full of apricots and he knows that

Stanhope dislikes this particular fruit. Osborne tries to reassure him. Just then Stanhope arrives, together with Second Lieutenant Trotter. Stanhope is angry about the condition of the trenches and orders Mason to bring him some whisky. When he is introduced to Raleigh, Stanhope is shocked to see him and an uneasy atmosphere descends, which Osborne tries his best to cover up.

Raleigh is introduced to Trotter and the men sit down to eat, although Stanhope becomes angry once more when they discover that there is no pepper to go with their soup. While they eat, they discuss their position and their duties for that night. Raleigh is sent on duty with Trotter as it is his first time in the trenches. The man they have relieved - Hibbert - enters the dugout, declines any food and, complaining of a pain in his eye, goes straight to bed. Stanhope seems to think that Hibbert is faking his illness and is unsympathetic. Osborne turns the conversation to Raleigh and Stanhope expresses his surprise that of all the Companies in France, Raleigh should have been sent to his. He shows Osborne a photograph of Raleigh's sister and tells him how concerned he is at how much his personality has changed and how frightened he is.

Stanhope reveals his fear that Raleigh will write to his sister, Madge and reveal the truth about his drinking. Then he realises that he could censor Raleigh's letters and continue to keep his drinking a secret. By now Stanhope is quite drunk and very tired, so Osborne persuades him to sleep for a while, and then retires to bed himself.

Main Points of Interest in Act One

HARDY'S ROLE
- Introduces humour right at the beginning of the play which sets the tone.
- Sets the scene by describing the surroundings, boredom and hardships in the dugout.
- Provides background information on Stanhope's character.

RALEIGH'S ARRIVAL
- Revealing conversation with Osborne regarding Stanhope's pre-war personality which differs greatly from Hardy's description.
- Raleigh's innocence and nervousness contrast with Hardy and Osborne who are more experienced and resigned to their situation.

MEETING BETWEEN RALEIGH AND STANHOPE
- Stanhope is shocked by Raleigh's arrival in his Company and reacts awkwardly.
- Raleigh's attempts at conversation are rejected by Stanhope.

STANHOPE'S CONVERSATION WITH OSBORNE
- Stanhope's resentment of Raleigh's presence becomes clear.
- He reveals his relationship with Madge to Osborne, showing that he trusts his friend more than Raleigh, with whom he has barely spoken.
- We learn of Stanhope's assessment of his own weaknesses and his fears for the future.

STANHOPE'S RELATIONSHIP WITH OSBORNE
- It is clear that Stanhope is closer to Osborne than to anyone else, including Raleigh.
- Stanhope is portrayed as 'childlike' and needy, while Osborne is seen as the 'father-figure' which is the opposite role to their ranks and experience.
- The audience learn how vital Osborne is to the Company as a whole and Stanhope in particular

ACT TWO

It is the following morning and Stanhope is on duty in the trench, while the other men are eating breakfast in the dugout. They talk about Stanhope, who they think looks unwell, although Raleigh seems embarrassed by the tone of the conversation and is reluctant to criticise his old friend. Sensing Raleigh's discomfort, Osborne changes the subject and they talk about the weather and gardening until Trotter goes to relieve Stanhope. Left by themselves for a short while, Osborne tells Raleigh that he used to play rugby for Harlequins and England, which impresses the younger man. They also discuss the war in general, although when Stanhope returns, Raleigh excuses himself and goes back to his own dugout to finish
a letter.

Osborne and Stanhope talk over their immediate tasks, such as repairing the barbed wire, and also the anticipated German attack. Although it is only early in the morning, Stanhope starts drinking. He is very worried about Raleigh's letter and when he reappears with it, ready for posting, Stanhope tells him that he must leave it open on the table so that it can be censored. Raleigh is flustered and initially refuses to show his letter, saying that he will leave it until later. This fuels Stanhope's fears and he wrenches the letter from Raleigh's hand in a violent outburst. Raleigh is shocked by his friend's behaviour and quietly leaves the dugout to go on duty. Osborne is also stunned, but Stanhope turns on him too, before realising that his actions were unnecessarily harsh. He no longer wants to read the letter and throws it down on the table. Osborne offers to glance at it, just to set Stanhope's mind at rest and reads it quietly to himself. When he has finished, he offers to tell Stanhope what Raleigh has said and, although he dreads hearing it, Stanhope agrees. Osborne reads part of Raleigh's letter aloud, which reveals that he feels honoured to be serving with Stanhope; that Stanhope is always tired, but that this is because he is such a good officer who rarely sleeps and is always trying to cheer up the men, and also that the men love him. Raleigh is full of pride that Stanhope is *his* friend. Osborne sticks down the envelope and Stanhope stands, ashamed now that he had doubted Raleigh.

Later that day, Stanhope is issuing instructions to a Sergeant-Major when the Colonel arrives. The Sergeant-Major is excused and then the Colonel reveals that he wants Stanhope to organise a raiding party to be sent across No Man's Land to capture one or two enemy soldiers, in the hope of discovering the strength of the opposition. The Colonel suggests that Osborne should lead the raid and be supported by Raleigh. Stanhope tries to convince the Colonel that Raleigh is too inexperienced, but eventually it is agreed that there is no-one else who could go and the Colonel leaves.

Hibbert appears, having been asleep. He says he feels too unwell to remain at the front. Stanhope tells him that he is suffering from the same complaint himself, but Hibbert persists, saying that he wants to leave the front line and go for medical assistance. Stanhope stops him and says that he will not be allowed to leave: he is not *that* unwell. Hibbert becomes hysterical and goes to collect his belongings, saying that he is going to leave anyway. Stanhope fetches his revolver and, when Hibbert returns and tries to leave the dugout, a heated argument follows during which Hibbert tries to hit Stanhope, who becomes angry and tells Hibbert that, rather than allow him to leave, he would shoot him and make it look like an accident. Hibbert tells him to go ahead - he would rather be shot than have to spend one more moment in the trenches. The two men face each other and eventually, Stanhope replaces his revolver and speaks quietly to Hibbert, telling him how frightened he is. He appeals to Hibbert not to let his comrades down and somehow persuades him to stay, offering to go on duty with him to help calm his nerves.

Osborne comes into the dugout and Stanhope tells him that he is to lead the raid. Stanhope leaves to make arrangements with the Sergeant-Major and a sleepy Trotter appears from his bed. Osborne tells him about the raid and they agree not to discuss the details in front of Raleigh in case he becomes frightened. Osborne is reading *Alice's Adventures in Wonderland* and Trotter seems surprised by his choice of book, although he has never read it himself.

Stanhope returns and collects Hibbert, taking him out into the trench. Osborne and Trotter settle down to some letter writing and Raleigh comes off duty, having been relieved by Stanhope and Hibbert. He has been told about the raid, and is very excited, viewing it as an adventurous opportunity.

Main Points of Interest in Act Two

CHARACTERS
- The audience learns more about Trotter and his background as well as what the others think about him.
- Stanhope wonders about his own sanity and is, once again, reassured by Osborne.
- We discover that Osborne has a family at home. Later in the scene, he demonstrates his loyalty to the Company.

THE LETTER
- Raleigh's reluctance to show his letter to Stanhope stems from his embarrassment at what he has written in praise of his hero.
- Stanhope's misinterpretation of this and his violent outburst reveal the extent of his paranoia.
- The contents of Raleigh's letter show his loyalty towards his old friend, as well as the high opinion in which Stanhope is held by his men. This shows us that Stanhope is much harsher towards himself than others.

THE COLONEL'S VISIT
- Brings the first news of the raid.
- Stanhope's reaction to the suggestion that Raleigh should go on the raid is interesting. He doesn't flinch when told Osborne is going, but tries several times to have Raleigh excused from this duty. This could suggest that he still feels responsible for Raleigh's welfare, or that he knows Raleigh's inexperience could prove costly.

STANHOPE'S ARGUMENT WITH HIBBERT
- Stanhope is portrayed as loyal, devoted to the whole Company and with high expectations of others, but ultimately sympathetic.
- Hibbert is shown as only interested in saving his own skin, but when this fails, his sole concern is that no-one should discover his weakness.

ACT THREE

It is the following afternoon and Stanhope is nervously pacing the floor of the dugout, when the Colonel arrives. The two men discuss the plans for the raid. When Osborne and Raleigh come in, the Colonel offers them words of encouragement. Once Osborne and Stanhope are alone, Osborne asks Stanhope to take care of his personal effects, just in case he does not come back from the raid. Stanhope says he will do this, but refuses to acknowledge that Osborne might not return. Finally, Raleigh and Osborne are alone and they go over what will happen during the raid. Then they try to talk about anything else *except* the raid, until eventually the time comes for them to leave. Raleigh suddenly seems nervous, but Osborne calms him down. They leave the dugout, which remains empty, although the noise of the raid can be heard.

When all has gone quiet, Stanhope and the Colonel come into the dugout from the trench. The raid has resulted in the capture of one German soldier who is brought down into the dugout. Stanhope goes back out to talk to the men, while the Colonel interrogates the prisoner. Stanhope returns and the Colonel absent-mindedly asks whether all the men have returned safely, to which Stanhope replies, bitterly, that Osborne and six others have been killed. Raleigh enters the dugout and, after congratulating him, the Colonel leaves. Raleigh sits, dumbfounded and in shock, on Osborne's bed. Stanhope has no words of consolation, but simply asks why he must sit there, rather than somewhere else.

Later that evening, Trotter, Stanhope and Hibbert, having dined, sit and tell stories and jokes. This has been a special dinner including chicken and champagne, but Raleigh has chosen to remain on duty in the trench, rather than join them. Hibbert reveals that Raleigh did not want to come to the dinner and preferred to be with the men. This news shakes Stanhope, who becomes angry and orders Hibbert to go to bed. Once they are alone, Stanhope tells Trotter that he is now second-in-command. Trotter promises not to disappoint Stanhope, and goes out to relieve Raleigh.

When Raleigh enters, Stanhope is angry with him for not attending the dinner and Raleigh makes matters worse by admitting that he has eaten with the men. Stanhope's temper becomes almost uncontrollable and Raleigh is confused, not just by Stanhope's attitude, but also about why they all had a celebratory meal when Osborne had just been killed. Stanhope angrily explains that the drinking and celebration are done to forget, not because he does not care. He dismisses Raleigh.

Very early the next morning, the officers wake up and prepare for the expected attack. Mason is told that he will have to join his platoon in the trench once he has completed his chores. The Sergeant-Major comes down to the dugout to get his instructions. Trotter comes out and calls for Raleigh and Hibbert to join him, before going out into the trench. Raleigh appears and pauses to say goodbye to Stanhope, who barely acknowledges him. Hibbert still has not appeared, so Stanhope calls him again, but when he does come out, he is reluctant to go into the trench. Eventually, Stanhope finds a way around the situation by asking Hibbert to accompany Mason into the trenches. Hibbert can hardly refuse this order and the two men leave. Various messages come down for Stanhope and he gets ready to go up himself. The Sergeant-Major comes down to tell him that Raleigh has been wounded. Stanhope tells him to bring Raleigh down to the dugout and, despite his surprise, the Sergeant-Major obeys and carries Raleigh to Osborne's bed. Raleigh has been badly wounded and Stanhope bathes his head. The two men talk briefly, although Raleigh does not understand the extent of his injuries. Stanhope conceals the truth from him and reassures him that he will be fine. Their friendship is restored as Stanhope briefly takes care of Raleigh in the few minutes before he dies.

A soldier comes down into the dugout and says that Trotter has asked for Stanhope to come up immediately. Stanhope pauses to touch Raleigh's head, before going up into the trench. Just as he does, a shell bursts just outside and the entrance caves in, extinguishing the one remaining candle. All is in darkness and the only sound is of the shells and machine-gun fire.

Main Points of Interest in Act Three

BEFORE THE RAID
- Stanhope's anxiety and sense of foreboding are clear.
- Osborne's and Stanhope's parting is a mixture of restraint and unspoken emotional intensity which sums up the difference between pre-war male roles and the close relationships that were formed during the conflict.
- Osborne's conversation with Raleigh demonstrates, once again, his importance to the Company.

AFTER THE RAID
- Osborne's death, by hand grenade as he waited for Raleigh, makes Stanhope bitter and angry as well as sad and reflective.
- Raleigh seeks help from Stanhope but is rejected. This may reflect Stanhope's feelings that Raleigh is somehow responsible for Osborne's death, or the fact that Stanhope simply cannot cope with someone else's grief and emotions.

THE DINNER
- Stanhope clearly does not want to talk about the raid, he wants to forget.
- Hibbert appears to be only concerned with having a good time - he has misinterpreted the reason behind the dinner.
- Stanhope's extreme anger towards Raleigh and his description of his feelings for Osborne show the audience how moved he really is to have lost his friend.

RECONCILIATION BETWEEN STANHOPE AND RALEIGH
- When Raleigh is wounded, Stanhope's insistence that he be brought to the dugout, his tender care for the dying man and, for the first time, his use of Raleigh's christian name all show how Stanhope really feels.
- Stanhope's character is restored and we glimpse his pre-war personality in this fleeting scene.

GLOSSARY OF TERMS

Some of the military language and terminology used in Journey's End can be confusing. We have included below a list of some of the terms or phrases from the play which may require explanation, in alphabetical order.

Billets - Lodging for a soldier, normally in a private home, farm outhouses or public buildings.

Boche - French slang for a German, also adopted by the British.

Dugout - A shelter dug underground. In the First World War, officers at the front essentially lived in these constructions which were sometimes joined together by a series of tunnels.

Funk - Fear or terror.

Lanyard - A cord worn around the waist or neck to secure a gun, knife or whistle.

Lewis Gun - A type of machine gun, used by the British during the First World War.

Log-book - The official record of what has taken place in a particular sector.

MC - Abbreviation for Military Cross. Established in December 1914, this medal was awarded for gallantry to officers, up to the rank of Captain, although it has since been expanded to include other ranks.

Minnies - A German trench mortar, actually named a 'Minenwerfer' which literally translates as 'mine-launcher'.

No Man's Land - Area of land between the front line trenches.

Parapet - The part of the trench which faces No Man's Land, raised to protect the men from enemy fire.

Pavé - French for a type of pavement, usually made of square cobbles on older roads.

Quartermaster-Sergeant - A senior non-commissioned officer who is responsible for supplies.

Sap - A communication trench dug at an angle from the main trench system.

Sentry Post - Position where a man could be positioned to stand guard or observe enemy activity.

Toch-emmas - Army slang for a trench mortar.

Trench Fever - A disease which was quite common in the First World War, causing high fever, headache an back or leg pain. It was transmitted by the lice that infested the men's clothing.

Very Lights - A flare fired from a gun.

Whizzbangs - Slang name used by the British for German artillery. Refers to the noise made by the travelling shell, followed by the explosion.

Wipers - Slang for the Belgian town of Ypres, which saw intense fighting throughout the First World War.

Characters

STANHOPE

The son of a country vicar, this young captain is the commanding officer of the company of men with whom Journey's End is concerned. Aged approximately twenty-one years, Stanhope has been in the trenches for almost three years, having gone into the army at eighteen. Physically, he is described as tall, thin, and having broad shoulders. The impression created is that he is fastidious about his appearance, having neatly brushed dark hair and a well-cared-for uniform. The description given of Stanhope also refers to the effects of serving in France for three years: although tanned, his face is pale and he appears very tired and drawn.

Even before his first appearance, the conversation between Osborne and Hardy has already made it clear that Stanhope drinks heavily and through the course of the play, we learn that this is done to boost his nerves, which even he appreciates, are shattered. The alcohol also helps him to forget the horrors of everyday trench life and death. This early conversation tells us much more about Stanhope; for example he is fussy about the cleanliness of the trenches. Stanhope likes the trenches and dugouts to be well maintained and with good reason: ammunition stored improperly in wet or damp trenches can go rusty and malfunction; disease can easily be spread amongst the men due to poor sanitation; and he resents the idea of his men, who already have sufficient tasks to keep them occupied, having to spend their time clearing up someone else's mess. To Stanhope, such inefficiency is intolerable. During this same conversation we also discover the high regard in which Stanhope is held. Osborne comments to Hardy that he does not know of anyone who is as good a commander as Stanhope and we learn how much Osborne loves him. Stanhope is obviously an excellent officer, and has been awarded the MC, so his courage is not in doubt to anyone except himself. He is concerned with the welfare of his men: but this concern, together with his experiences and fears have taken their toll on him both physically and mentally. He is a man on the verge of breaking down.

When his old friend Raleigh appears in his Company, Stanhope is shocked and he finds it difficult to disguise this. Ever since they were at school together Stanhope has always regarded it as his responsibility to look after Raleigh, particularly as their fathers were old friends. Now his task is harder than ever - taking care of a younger boy at school, and living up to his high expectations is completely different from looking after a junior officer in the front line trenches. He is also aware that Raleigh has always hero-worshipped him, and he is afraid of losing Raleigh's respect once it becomes clear how drastically different he has become.

He would prefer it if Raleigh had been able to remember him as a boy-hood hero, than a broken man, which is how Stanhope now perceives himself. In addition he is also concerned that in writing home, Raleigh will betray Stanhope's altered nature and that this might not only shatter his image within his own family, but also with Raleigh's sister Madge, who he obviously loves and with whom he has an understanding. He is keen that Raleigh's sister should be proud of him, and never know of the ways in the which the war has changed him. It is also possible that Stanhope is finding it almost impossible to reconcile his pre-war life with his wartime existence. Seeing Raleigh simply reminds him of a life he has left behind. Watching Raleigh's reactions to the changed Stanhope also reinforces Stanhope's opinion that he is become so badly affected by the war that he will be unrecognisable afterwards.

Stanhope's outburst when Raleigh refuses to hand over his letter is extreme and shocks his young friend, as well as Osborne, who has clearly never seen Stanhope behave in this way before. However, Stanhope soon realises that he has behaved badly and his reaction to the content of Raleigh's letter shows how ashamed he is of his own shortcomings. This episode also demonstrates to the audience that, despite his own poor opinion of himself, Stanhope is still essentially a decent man.

Stanhope is conscious of the impression he creates with his men and junior officers and the only person allowed to see him with his guard down is Osborne. Stanhope is very critical of himself but his opinion of his own shortcomings is not reflected by the men in his own Company, who, despite his obvious problems, continue to look up to and respect him. This is not a universally-held opinion, as we have already learned from Hardy that some of the men from outside his company regard Stanhope's behaviour as somewhat freakish or laughable, especially when he is drunk. This may be, however, because it is easier for them to laugh at him than to appreciate that what has happened to him could just as easily happen to them.

We also see that Stanhope is a man with a strong sense of duty: while discussing plans with the Sergeant-Major, he suggests that, rather than retreat in the face of the enemy, the company will continue to go forward until they have won the war! This is said half-humourously - Stanhope obviously has no intention of retreating - it would be contrary to his orders, but also he wants to reassure the Sergeant-Major who seems to be worried about the strength of the anticipated attack.

Hibbert's supposed illness demonstrates another side of Stanhope, who makes it clear that he will do whatever it takes for the good of his Company. This becomes clear in the episode where Hibbert attempts to evade further participation in the forthcoming attack. Stanhope initially threatens to shoot Hibbert - a fate which would have befallen him anyway, had he deserted. Then, when Hibbert breaks down, Stanhope tells him that he is experiencing exactly the same fears himself. In threatening to shoot Hibbert, we can see that Stanhope places the morale and well-being of the whole company above that of any one man, including himself. If Hibbert had been allowed to carry on behaving as he was, his duties would have suffered and the men might be put at risk as a consequence a chance which Stanhope is not prepared to take. Stanhope is also aware that, by leaving, Hibbert would be placing an unfair burden on the officers left behind. He also knows that in the long run, it will be better for Hibbert to stay and face the enemy than run and never know if his courage would have failed him at the vital moment.

Stanhope reveals his own fears to Hibbert both as a means of shaming the junior officer into staying and also to make him realise that feeling terrified is quite common and is nothing of which to be ashamed. This is an interesting point to note as earlier on, he had been worried that Raleigh's letter home might reveal his own fears and perceived weaknesses. Stanhope, it would seem, is more tolerant and forgiving of other people's defects than of his own. It is also worth noting that Stanhope never reveals Hibbert's actions to anyone, which demonstrates his loyalty to his men.

The news of the planned raid hits Stanhope hard. Initially he offers to take part himself, and then tries to persuade the Colonel that Raleigh is unsuited to the task, which may show that he still feels responsible for his old schoolfriend, or that he is concerned that Raleigh's lack of experience may put the raiding party at unneccesary risk. The Colonel, however, refuses to be swayed - he cannot spare Stanhope, and there really is no-one else who can accompany Osborne. Stanhope is clearly worried at having to send anyone on this mission, which he feels is not worth risking the lives of his men.

When Stanhope and Osborne part, there is an unspoken intensity of feeling between them, which is shown in the glances between them and awkward pauses in their conversation. Stanhope agrees to take care of Osborne's belongings but will not acknowledge the possibility that his friend might not return from the raid. He quite rightly points out that he would be lost without Osborne.

When Osborne is killed, Stanhope is bitter and angry and these are feelings which he takes out on Raleigh, who has returned safely, although this could also be because he knows that Osborne was killed while waiting for Raleigh and perhaps he feels that Raleigh is responsible for Osborne's death. He acknowledges to Raleigh that in losing Osborne, he has lost his best friend and the one person in whom he could confide - he is unsure of how he will be able to continue without his "Uncle" by his side. He attempts to mask his emotions once again, by drinking and laughing with Trotter and Hibbert, but eventually reveals his true feelings in another angry outburst against Raleigh.

When his old schoolfriend is injured Stanhope reverts to his real personality, trying to spare Raleigh the knowledge of his impending death. This is the real Stanhope, as he was before he became damaged by his experiences in the war. He tenderly cares for Raleigh and looks after him to the very end. His status as hero is restored - both to Raleigh and to himself: he has done his duty.

Stanhope has a complex character; a strange entwinement of pre-war reticence and wartime raw emotions. Before the war, Stanhope would have been a man who others respected for his strength, bravery, sportsmanship and gentlemanly behaviour. He feels that all of these qualities are now lost to him and no longer seems to understand his own feelings because they are so foreign to him. It is almost impossible for us, in the 21st century, to understand the emotional, physical and psychological trauma of a conflict like the First World War, but we must also understand that before the war there was a code of conduct for men of Stanhope's class and background which did not involve showing one's emotions or expressing one's feelings. The character of Stanhope that we see in Journey's End is a microcosm of the impact of the First World War on every aspect of life - everything had changed and nothing would ever be the same again.

In creating this character, Sherriff had looked to generate someone whom others would look up to: a leader and a hero, worthy of Raleigh's worship. However, he also wanted to depict that the war could wreak havoc on a man, even as gallant and seemingly "perfect" as Stanhope. He wanted those in the audience who had lived through the war to be able to relate to Stanhope's personality and reactions, so he presented him with a series of problems and issues, such as Hibbert's refusal to fight and Osborne's death and then showed the audience that, despite his own personal despair, Stanhope would still rise above it all and do the right thing. Sherriff also needed the audience to appreciate the depths to which Stanhope had fallen, by depicting Raleigh's reactions to him and his recollections of Stanhope as his schoolboy hero. In this way, Sherriff is able to show the path which Stanhope has taken - from the innocent sporting heroic boy of school days, to the broken, confused and ultimately still courageous young man at his Journey's End..

Colin Keith-Johnston as Captain Stanhope in Journey's End
at the Henry Miller Theatre, New York, March 22, 1929.

Photograph courtesy of NYPL Digital Gallery. Digital ID: 499286

RALEIGH

Raleigh is the innocent young recruit who arrives, excited at being involved in the war, and particularly at being able to serve under his old schoolboy hero, Stanhope. He is described as a handsome, healthy, but somewhat naive and inexperienced young man.

Upon first arriving, Raleigh is nervous and eager to please, although unsure of how he is supposed to behave. He talks enthusiastically to Osborne of his pre-war friendship with "Dennis" Stanhope. He reveals that he has used his uncle, General Raleigh's, influence to achieve this posting, because he desperately wanted to serve under his old schoolfriend. This is probably partly because Stanhope has always taken care of him and Raleigh hopes this will continue at the front, but also because he simply worships Stanhope and desperately wants to be with him, and follow in his footsteps.

Despite Osborne's friendly warnings about the effect that three years fighting has had on Stanhope, Raleigh is still surprised by Stanhope's appearance and his less than enthusiastic welcome. It is as though Raleigh had expected their relationship to be exactly the same as it was when they were at school. Upon first witnessing Stanhope's drunkenness, Raleigh appears shocked and seems to prefer not to be in company with his old friend, choosing instead to go into his own dugout. This may be because he senses that Stanhope resents his presence, but also could be a symptom of denial - Raleigh simply cannot believe that his old friend could be so badly affected, when everyone at home has always believed him to be coping so well with the war.

Stanhope's reaction to his letter also comes as a blow to Raleigh. He had not anticipated that his letter would need to be censored, presumably because he feels that Stanhope should trust him and he is embarrassed by the prospect of Stanhope reading the contents of his letter. Stanhope misreads Raleigh's reluctance and reacts violently towards him. Raleigh seems to understand the effects of the war on Stanhope, but is still confused, and disappointed by his friend's reaction. In this letter, however, he reveals nothing of Stanhope's changed nature, but remains loyal himself, pointing out instead how hardworking and tireless Stanhope is and that he is an excellent and well-respected officer. He finishes by telling his family of his pride in the knowledge that Stanhope is his friend.

On hearing that he is to help lead the raiding party, Raleigh is nervously enthusiastic. As the hour approaches, his nerves begin to dominate his enthusiasm and it is Osborne, rather than Stanhope, who comforts him. His youth and inexperience are revealed in this scene as he talks nervously to Osborne, trying not to dwell on the raid, refusing to have rum in his coffee and pointing out that he has never smoked a cigar before. This also emphasises the difference in age between the two men, with Raleigh seeming, more than ever, like the schoolboy while Osborne is the wise, kind and inspiring "school teacher".

After the raid, when Osborne is dead, Raleigh is clearly in shock and can barely stand up as he speaks to the Colonel. This new experience has made him understand the horror of the war - something which Stanhope had obviously wanted to spare him for as long as possible. Raleigh needs Stanhope's help and support, but receives neither as Stanhope is incapable of dealing with Raleigh's feelings - he is struggling with his own.

Raleigh's decision to remain in the trenches with the men, rather than join in the dinner demonstrates that he has not fully understood the etiquette of the dugout. Despite the impression that the officers are celebrating, they are for the best part, trying to forget what has happened - to drown their sorrows. In addition, Raleigh had noted in his letter than Stanhope spent a great deal of time with the men in the trenches trying to cheer them up and ease their fears. Perhaps by remaining in the trenches he is trying to emulate his hero - to please him and relieve him of the worry of looking after the men. This backfires as Stanhope is angry with Raleigh for having missed the dinner. He takes it as a personal slight to himself and the other officers. During their argument Raleigh comes to realise how much Osborne had meant to Stanhope. He feels left out of Stanhope's thoughts and doesn't understand his reactions. He wants to be involved and to help Stanhope, but cannot because his friend will not communicate with him. Raleigh would prefer to talk about his feelings, both for Osborne and for Stanhope, but Stanhope rejects this overture, angrily pushing Raleigh away.

Ultimately, the only time that Raleigh is able to recapture the old Stanhope, is on his death-bed, as we get a glimpse of what their relationship once was. His hero looks after him and ensures that he feels safe, comfortable and unafraid.

Overall there is an awkwardness between Raleigh and Stanhope because Raleigh had assumed that by being with Stanhope, everything would be as it had been at school. He has also failed to understand that the war has changed Stanhope to such an extent - he remembers his friend as a young dashing officer, keen to join the fight, and barely recognises the man he has become. Stanhope, on the other hand, resents Raleigh's presence as a reminder of his old life and the person he once was. In addition, Stanhope has formed new friendships now, especially with Osborne, who he looks up to and respects. These are not the sort of feelings he can have for Raleigh whose innocence represents everything he has lost.

Sherriff had several purposes in creating the role of Raleigh. Firstly, he wanted to demonstrate the central theme of hero-worship - a subject which many in his audience would have related to quite easily. He also wanted to depict the immediate impact of war, to show that just one bad experience could change the character and perspective of a man. In this way, the audience not only gains a greater understanding of lost youth, but also of someone like Stanhope, who has seen so much more than Raleigh, but manages to survive.

Raleigh's presence is vital to the depiction of Stanhope's character, but he also represents a type of his own, namely the young men, who even late in the war had retained their eagerness and raw innocence, despite the lengthening casualty lists.

Raleigh's passage and the development of his character come about through a few separate episodes. Firstly he sees the change in Stanhope, which shocks him, but he remains loyal to his own friend. Then, when Raleigh writes his letter and is faced with Stanhope's anger (possibly for the first time in his life), he is stunned by the reaction he receives. Even then, he knows that deep down, Stanhope is still a decent man. The raid is really the turning point for Raleigh. It is his first experience of war and death, but his survival and Osborne's death provide the audience with some scenes of high emotion, between Raleigh and Stanhope, from which the young subaltern would possibly never have recovered. Stanhope's reaction to Osborne's death and his treatment of Raleigh change the dynamic of their friendship but, at the moment of his death, Sherriff allows Raleigh to see the return of his hero. He can die in peace, knowing that his friend did, indeed, care for and look after him until the end and that his faith in Stanhope was justified.

OSBORNE

While significantly older than Stanhope, Osborne is junior in rank. Married, with two children, he is physically tough and rugged - the opposite of his personality which is level-headed, friendly and trusting. His feelings for his family are clear when he tells Stanhope that he spent the whole of his last leave at home with them, not even going to see any shows. He describes with great warmth the peaceful evenings spent with his wife and playing at soldiers with his two sons. His choice of reading material is interesting: *Alice's Adventures in Wonderland* presumably reminds him of happier times at home with his children. However, once he is back at the front, the Company become his family.

Osborne is very protective of Stanhope, trying to help him wherever possible. Their relationship is not based on hero-worship: Osborne knows and appreciates Stanhope's faults but his respect for his senior officer is borne out of years of experience and time spent with Stanhope at the front. Osborne realises that being in command brings with it heavy responsibilities and he knows that these have taken their toll on Stanhope; despite this, however, Stanhope has remained an excellent and diligent officer, and it is this which earns him Osborne's love and respect. He defends Stanhope's actions to Raleigh and especially Hardy, showing his loyalty to his commanding officer.

Osborne is very kind to Raleigh, who is nervous when he first arrives. He tries to warn Raleigh that Stanhope has changed and also attempts to deflect Raleigh's hero-worship by pointing out that he had played rugby for Harlequins and England. This is not done in a boastful manner, but more as a means of diverting Raleigh's attention from Stanhope, who he knows will be troubled by Raleigh's presence. He is not a vain man which he demonstrates when Hardy suggests that he would make a better Commanding Officer than Stanhope - a suggestion which he adamantly refutes.

As a former schoolmaster, Osborne is used to looking after boys, and his position in the dugout seems to be an extension of this role, to the point where he is nicknamed "Uncle". The use of this name gives Osborne an air of homeliness and reliability, which helps to make the atmosphere in the dugout seem less oppressive. He is always on hand with sensible advice and words of wisdom and is keen to avoid conflict within the dugout. It is always Osborne who helps Stanhope, especially when he is drunk, or over-tired. His first concern is to protect his Commanding Officer from the prying eyes and judgement of others, but also from the most destructive influence in Stanhope's life - himself. Within this role, he takes the decision to read Raleigh's letter to Stanhope, fully understanding that Stanhope must know the contents or he will dwell on what Raleigh might have written. In reading this letter, Osborne's self-effacing nature is demonstrated as he appears embarrassed by Raleigh's praise of him.

Osborne is very diplomatic: for example, his method of getting Mason to wash the dish-cloth is to ask his wife to send him out some soap powder and then suggest to Mason that he might like to try using it. Also when there is obviously a problem with Hibbert, Osborne deflects Trotter's enquiries and changes the subject. When Stanhope suggests that he will deface Trotter's chart of circles by drawing a picture of Trotter being blown up at the time when the attack is anticipated, Osborne dissuades him. This is not because he can really see the point behind Trotter's chart, but because he knows that Trotter had spent a considerable amount of time producing it in the first place and would be offended to have his chart ruined. Maybe, however, unlike Stanhope, Osborne realises that Trotter will see the significance of the drawing and knows that, as such, it will only add to the tension within the dugout. He understands that some of the men need to be able to look on the bright side of things and that Trotter hopes they will survive the attack and go back down the line again, even if Stanhope believes that is impossible.

His reaction upon being told that he is to lead the raid, and his desire not to talk about it beforehand, demonstrate that he is wary of being sent on this mission. He is an officer of some experience and has been on raids before, but now he seems to have a sense of his own mortality as he gives his belongings to Stanhope for safe-keeping, to be returned to his wife should he not survive. He manages to overcome his own fear, at least for appearance's sake, and calms the nerves of Raleigh, who has never experienced anything like this before and, as the hour approaches, becomes more and more nervous.

Osborne's attitude towards the men is always caring and considerate and although he is an officer of some standing, he has not yet become war-weary, like Stanhope. He has a sensible yet realistic perspective of the war and his duty.

Osborne's death signifies a change for this small group of officers. Raleigh, who was with him at the time, feels guilty and disturbed by Osborne's death, while Stanhope has lost the one fellow officer he knew he could trust implicitly. Even if the attack had not happened the next morning, one senses that this Company of men would never have been quite the same again.

Osborne is a pivotal personality in the play. Quite often it is through his eyes that the audience sees the traits of other characters. This is especially the case in the conversation between Osborne and Hardy about Stanhope. Here, not only do we discover that Stanhope is admired and respected by the men with whom he actually serves (as opposed to those who merely know him by reputation), but we also learn of Osborne's 'love' for Stanhope. His use of this word to describe his feelings shows his emotional maturity. He is not afraid to express himself or that he will be misunderstood; he knows and can explain, if necessary, that his love is platonic. He doesn't mind Hardy making fun of him, because he knows that his relationship with Stanhope is more important. Raleigh's reactions to Stanhope are also enhanced by Osborne, who helps the new arrival to come to terms with the changes in his old school friend. Sherriff's portrayal of Osborne in this way allows the audience to see his respect for such officers, who provided a father-figure for their juniors, both in terms of age and rank. At the same time, we see that Sherriff is demonstrating the depth of emotion that was possible between the men in the trenches. Osborne is shown to be the 'glue' that holds this group of officers together and the consequences of his death threaten to split them apart.

Unlike some of the other characters, Osborne is not really shown to develop during the play, because he must be seen as the one stable force in the group, who guides the others through everything. Only in this way can Sherriff allow the audience to understand the feelings of loss that came with the death of such a valued man.

TROTTER

Trotter is not in the best physical shape - he is rotund and red-faced. He is also middle-aged with a bursting tunic - the result, no doubt, of too much indulgence in his favourite interest - the consumption of food. He is married and his letters to his wife and descriptions of his home life, such as his garden, serve to remind us that all of these men have something to live for, and so much to lose.

He is a friendly, tolerant character, who is supportive of his fellow officers and loyal to Stanhope. He is also concerned about Stanhope's drinking and health, although he does not have the same close relationship as his Commanding Officer shares with Osborne. His concerns for Stanhope could stem from his fears that if Stanhope becomes too unstable, the Company could be put at risk. Unlike the other officers, Trotter has been promoted through the ranks and, this would give him a better impression of the men's needs with regards to strong leadership. In addition he may be worried that if Stanhope has to be replaced by another officer, the Company will lose its identity as a unit.

Trotter, presumably, does not have the same public school background as the other officers, which is demonstrated by the fact that his language is more colloquial than theirs. Outwardly, Trotter appears to be very unemotional, but the impression is given that this is only on the surface and that Trotter's feelings go much deeper than it would seem. In fact, when Stanhope says that he envies Trotter for being able to maintain a sense of normality, Trotter makes it clear that this is most definitely not the case. He doesn't like to talk about how he feels, using humour to overcome difficult circumstances, and therefore he falsely creates the impression that he doesn't worry about anything - that everything is a joke, but maybe this is just a mask to hide his own fears in the only way he knows.

Stanhope, while liking Trotter, feels that he lacks imagination: he believes that he and Osborne look more deeply at life, while Trotter merely observes what is on the surface. This demonstrates one of the perceived differences between their classes. They have drive and ambition, while Trotter is happy with his lot in life. This is reinforced later on, when he points out that he has never owned a car, but that he and his wife used to walk everywhere together, but he does not seem to resent the fact that others have more than him.

After Osborne's death, Trotter becomes Stanhope's second-in-command, but this brief relationship is more formal than Stanhope and Osborne's had been. Trotter feels honoured by the promotion and promises not to let Stanhope down. He is an honourable and decent man. Even on the final morning, immediately before the dreaded attack, Trotter appears cheerful - he sings songs while in his dugout which helps to relieve the feeling of tension and probably also serves to take his own mind off what might lie ahead.

Some critics describe Trotter as an artificial character - somewhat unnecessary to the plot. This does him a grave injustice as his importance lies in the subtleties of what he says: his reactions demonstrate the common feeling. So, for example, he's worried about the raid - even though he is not involved - but he knows that it is useless to argue, as the orders will not be revoked, no matter how pointless and costly the raid might be. He knows that nothing he can do will change the course of the war, but equally he does not see why he should have to suffer more discomfort than is absolutely necessary. Much of the humour in the play emanates from Trotter and centres on his love of food. Not only does he joke about things, but the others make fun of him, although this is never done offensively, but in friendship.

Sherriff portrays Trotter as the ordinary man, who has answered his country's call and gone to war to do his duty. By showing him as someone who has risen through the ranks, Sherriff is reminding the audience that many of the officers had actually come from working or middle class backgrounds, but had achieved the same status as the others through hard work. These men were given the somewhat unfair title of 'temporary gentlemen', suggesting that they were not really considered to be good enough to associate with the upper class officers on a permanent basis, while also reminding them that their position of 'gentleman' only held good for the duration of the war. By making Trotter such a good-natured and likeable man, Sherriff is probably expressing his distaste for this treatment of such men.

Sherriff uses Trotter to inject humour, but also humanity, into the play. Trotter is the mild-mannered, quiet and ordinary men, who represents the everyday person, seeing everything, but not necessarily commenting on it.

As the play progresses, Trotter's character develops a little. While he remains humorous, for the best part, right until the end, the audience is given greater and greater glimpses of the quieter and more thoughtful side of Trotter's nature. After Osborne's death, he does his best to help Stanhope, without trying to replace Osborne, even though his advice is not always welcomed. Initially, when we first see Trotter, the main focus of his attention is on food, but as time progresses, we see that he has a much deeper and more thoughtful personality, often showing his consideration for the other officers in quiet and unobtrusive ways.

HIBBERT

Hibbert is a young, slightly obscure man with a pale face - reminiscent of a weasel - both in appearance and manner. First impressions of Hibbert are not good. He complains of feeling unwell almost continuously and craves escape from the trenches.

Hibbert doesn't initially interact with his fellow-officers, although he knows them all well, having been with them for approximately three months. Instead he prefers to sleep and keep his own company whenever he is not on duty, although one gets the impression that he may be doing this to support his argument that he is unwell.

During his quarrel with Stanhope, it becomes clear that Hibbert is terrified of going back into the trenches and is persuaded to stay only by Stanhope first threatening and then sympathising with him. This exchange shows Hibbert in an unfavourable light and although he agrees to stay, he then becomes concerned that Stanhope might tell the others of his cowardice. This confirms that Stanhope had been right in his assumption that Hibbert was faking his physical illness, and also shows that Hibbert is a shallow man whose sole concerns are his own welfare and reputation, rather than the well-being of the Company as a whole.

This bad impression is exacerbated by his reaction to Osborne's death. Whereas for Trotter and Stanhope, the meal and light conversation are a means to forget, Hibbert uses this opportunity to show off his lewd postcards and boast of his exploits with women - he simply wants to enjoy himself. He also gossips about Raleigh, passing information to Stanhope, which shows he does not share the common sense of loyalty, which he seems to expect of others. Stanhope's distaste for Hibbert is obvious throughout the play, but really comes out in this scene.

When the time comes to go back into the trenches, Hibbert is again hesitant and fearful. In fact he has to be called several times before appearing on the morning of the final attack. He seems unwilling to go up into the trenches, wasting a great deal of time and making excuses, until Stanhope tells him to accompany Mason. This is Stanhope's way of shaming Hibbert into doing his duty - if Mason can do it, so can he. Although this works and Hibbert goes, he hesitates again and, unlike all the others, does not say anything to Stanhope.

The portrayal of Hibbert is, perhaps, one of the most interesting aspects of the play. Most people have assumed, down the years, that Sherriff based the characters on people that he knew and met during the war and in most instances, this is the case. In his letters home from the trenches, he describes some of his fellow officers and some of their characteristics can be seen within the personalities included in the play, although they are almost all combinations of several different people. The case of Hibbert is no exception but the source for his inspiration is quite surprising. In some of his letters, Sherriff complains of having neuralgia and of making requests to be sent back down the line for treatment. He speaks of his fear and the fact that his nerves quite often get the better of him. Although he never shirked his duties, or showed off lewd postcards, it would seem that some of Hibbert's characteristics are autobiographical.

Hibbert's main purpose in the play is to show us how Stanhope reacts to being placed in difficult situations. In Hibbert's company, we see Stanhope angry, impatient, sympathetic, disgusted and irritated. Hibbert has a tendency to bring out the worst in others, but Stanhope still tries his best to show strong leadership, demonstrating understanding for Hibbert's nerves and fears. The audience is not necessarily supposed to sympathise with, or even like Hibbert: he is there to help us understand the traits of others and show how two different men, under the same stresses, will react in contrasting ways. As such, the audience grows to appreciate Stanhope even more.

Hibbert becomes even less likeable after Osborne's death and this development helps the audience to understand how much the loss of Osborne will affect the Company. Hibbert's behaviour is inappropriate and he shows himself to be selfish and inconsiderate, providing a good contrast with the other remaining officers.

Even at the end, Hibbert hasn't changed. He doesn't want to go up into the trench and tries to delay. Stanhope's reaction to this is the most important aspect, but the fact that they part without speaking shows that, despite his best efforts, Stanhope has achieved nothing in his attempts to make Hibbert a better, more considerate and more understanding officer. Within this depiction, Sherriff may well have been trying to reveal that, sometimes the war didn't alter or make men - sometimes they were just who they had always been.

MASON

Mason is essentially a servant and his general responsibility is to take care of the officers to whom he is assigned. He cooks their meals and clears up after them. This does not, however, mean that he escapes the fighting - he must also take part in any battles in which his company are involved.

Although we are told little about Mason's appearance or personality, we can conclude that he is hard working, loyal and caring. He never questions his orders, and is keen to please. For example, prior to the final battle, he makes sandwiches for the officers, before going up into the trenches. Mason is often the butt of light-hearted jokes about food and cooking, but this is done without malice.

When Stanhope suggests that Hibbert and Mason go up into the trench together, Mason appears grateful, which may demonstrate his own nervousness. This could, however, be interpreted as showing Mason's understanding of the real situation surrounding Hibbert and his desire to be useful to Stanhope.

The role of Mason's character in the play is to provide humorous respite in the building tension, his interactions with Trotter being particularly amusing. He also serves to remind us that, for the officers in the dugout, in spite of their surroundings and horrific experiences, ordinary activities still go on. The men must eat, and the discussion of what they are eating and how it has been cooked provides a useful diversion from the war, and in many cases, helps to enhance the human qualities of the play.

Although, for the main part of the play, Mason's role revolves around his kitchen duties, at the end we get to see that he must also fight and this serves to remind us that he is also still a soldier, with the same worries and fears as everyone else. Sherriff clearly wanted his audience to understand that the humour was a mask to allow Mason to get through each day.

HARDY

Hardy is a Captain, who commands the company from whom Stanhope's men are taking over. It would seem that he has been at the front for some time, as nothing really seems to surprise him. His role in the play is to set the scene. His conversation with Osborne serves the purpose of explaining the anticipated attack, and Stanhope's personality, as well as some of the boredom and routine of trench-life. We also learn that the opinion of other officers regarding Stanhope's personality is very different from that of his loyal Osborne.

Hardy is a humourous, philosophical character, who has a light-hearted outlook on almost everything, including the general hardships of the war, although this might be more obvious as he is being relieved and going behind the lines - whether he would be as amused if he were the one coming into the trenches is another matter.

This initial scene involving Hardy helps to set the tone for the rest of the play, and helps the reader or audience appreciate that this black humour was an important aspect of life in the trenches. During this scene, as well as learning about the still absent Stanhope, we also learn a great deal about Osborne and how well-respected he is amongst the other men - even those not in his own Company.

RELATIONSHIPS

Being as *Journey's End* is set entirely within the tight confines of a small dugout, the relationships portrayed between the characters involved become vitally important to the audience's understanding of the play. Some of the relationships are more crucial than others, but even the more minor ones can be used to help demonstrate some of the themes within this piece.

STANHOPE AND OSBORNE

This is probably the most important and complex relationship in the play. Osborne takes care of Stanhope, looking after him when he is drunk and making sure that he gets enough rest. He is also very protective of Stanhope, defending his behaviour to Hardy and explaining that Stanhope's experiences have made him the way he is. During Osborne's conversation with Hardy, he makes it clear that Stanhope keeps nothing from him. Hardy reveals an episode that he considers to be embarrassing and detrimental to Stanhope, and is then surprised when Osborne explains that he was already aware of what had taken place because Stanhope had told him all about it himself. The trust between Osborne and Stanhope is obvious from that moment on and is enhanced by the fact that Stanhope later shares his fears that Raleigh will write home to his family and tell them how much Stanhope has changed. Again Osborne shows his concern, explaining that Raleigh wouldn't do this and trying to calm Stanhope's worries.

Although Stanhope is the senior officer and has seen more service, he doesn't really issue Osborne with orders in the same way as the other men and treats him as more of an equal. Because Osborne is older, he takes on the role of father-figure, offering sound advice to Stanhope whenever he over-reacts. At the same time, Osborne looks up to Stanhope, appreciating his qualities as an officer and leader, while realising that he always puts everyone else ahead of himself. It is this mutual respect and affection which makes this relationship more interesting and realistic.

Even though Osborne holds Stanhope in high esteem, he is not always full of praise for his captain's actions and Stanhope doesn't simply bow down to everything that Osborne says. When Stanhope first mentions censoring Raleigh's letter, Osborne is taken aback. Both men know that Stanhope has every right to do this, but Osborne feels that it shows an unjustified lack of trust in Stanhope's former schoolfriend. The real crunch comes when Raleigh has actually written his letter and Stanhope snatches it from him, using an unnecessary amount of force. Afterwards, Osborne reads Raleigh's letter aloud to Stanhope, not to prove him wrong, so much as to show him that he should have more faith - not only in Raleigh, but also in himself. Osborne's protective attitude towards Stanhope comes out in this scene. He could just have left the letter for Stanhope to read alone, but he really wanted Stanhope to realise the consequences of continuing to push Raleigh away.

There is a strong emotional connection between the two men which is made clear right at the very beginning of the play when Osborne explains to Hardy that he loves Stanhope. This is not a homosexual love and neither is it as simple as the love between two friends. The bonds formed in the trenches were often more powerful and the relationships stronger than even those between a husband and wife and that is the type of 'love' which Osborne is describing here. He is being quite serious when he comments that he would 'go to hell' with Stanhope and the strength of their relationship is made more obvious by the descriptions of Osborne's time with his family, which is given the air of something more comforting and homely, rather than being as powerful and intense as his time with Stanhope.

Stanhope's fear of losing Osborne is made clear before the raid as he wonders 'what [he] would do' without his 'Uncle', while only grudgingly accepting Osborne's belongings to pass on to his wife, refusing to acknowledge that Osborne might not survive. There is a slightly lighthearted tone to this scene, but the undercurrent is highly emotional, as deep down, both men understand the seriousness of the situation, even though neither really wants to face it. Osborne's death is devastating for Stanhope, to the point where he can't bear to see Raleigh sitting on Osborne's bed. Although Stanhope joins in the dinner with Trotter and Hibbert that evening, he does so to 'forget', not to celebrate or remember and he later flares up at Raleigh, explaining vehemently that by Osborne's death he has lost 'the one man [he] could trust', the man who 'understood everything', who he considered as his 'best friend'.

Sherriff's portrayal of this relationship is especially useful in demonstrating the strength of feelings which were felt between the men in the trenches. The trust which developed was rarely found elsewhere and nowhere within the play can this be seen any better. The relationship between Stanhope and Osborne also shows the family element of the play in that Osborne is very much the father-figure, as well as being everyone's 'Uncle'. Although he is not the senior officer, he is very much the one to whom everyone looks for advice and good sense and, despite the fact that Stanhope is his senior, he does not resent the respect shown to Osborne.

Although it could be argued that we do not really see a development in this relationship, that might be because we don't really need to. The strength of feeling between the two men is already so powerful and remains so until the end. The only real development required, therefore, is the feeling of loss which Stanhope has to suffer after Osborne's death, which is made palpable by his need to forget and also by his reactions to his old schoolfriend, Raleigh.

STANHOPE AND RALEIGH

Of all the relationships in *Journey's End*, the one between Stanhope and Raleigh is the only one which has any basis outside of the war and the confines of the play itself. At school, with Stanhope having been a few years older than Raleigh and a popular, sporting student, the younger boy had looked up to Stanhope as his hero. Raleigh's arrival in Stanhope's Company takes him by surprise, but this emotion soon turns to fear, laced with anger, as Stanhope reveals to Osborne his concern that Raleigh will write to his sister and tell her how much Stanhope has changed. The prospect of this is upsetting for Stanhope, as is the idea that he must crush Raleigh's perceptions of him as a hero. Stanhope appreciates that Raleigh's presence will place him under even more strain as not only must he try to appear normal to the youngster, but he still feels the need to protect him. This aspect comes to the fore when the Colonel proposes that Raleigh should accompany Osborne on the raid. Stanhope had made no comment about sending Osborne out, but when Raleigh's name is suggested, he objects, making excuses as to why he shouldn't go.

Raleigh is very naive about his relationship with Stanhope and expects it to be just as it was at school. He thinks that their previous connection and shared memories still count for something because he doesn't realise the strain that Stanhope is under or how much the war has changed him. The hero-worship that Stanhope feels for Raleigh doesn't really diminish, placing even more pressure on Stanhope, although a lot of this is self-imposed as Stanhope sets himself very high standards.

There are two episodes that change the relationship between Raleigh and Stanhope. The first is their exchange over Raleigh's letter; the second is Osborne's death. When Raleigh withdraws his letter because he doesn't want Stanhope to read it, Stanhope automatically assumes the worst - that Raleigh has written to Madge, telling her of his downfall. Stanhope's angry reaction stuns Raleigh and, for the first time, he really sees Stanhope in a new light. Of course, once Stanhope realises that Raleigh has only written in praise of him and that his reluctance of have his letter censored was due to embarrassment, he appreciates that his reaction has now caused precisely the damage he had been hoping to avoid. Any chance Stanhope might have had of retaining Raleigh's inspired good opinion is now lost and he regrets his outburst on many levels. After this episode, Raleigh becomes a little more guarded in his attitude towards Stanhope.

Osborne's death has an even more dramatic effect on this relationship. Stanhope's response is surprising to Raleigh, in that he joins the other officers in a special meal. Raleigh, meanwhile, chooses to remain in the trench with the men, sharing their rations. Raleigh's actions anger Stanhope, but equally the younger man cannot understand how Stanhope can laugh and drink following the death of his friend. This episode highlights the differences that exist between the two men and how much their relationship has changed since they were at school. When Stanhope reveals his true feelings for Osborne, Raleigh is lost. For the first time, he realises that Stanhope is not as strong as he had thought an that he needs people too. The fact that Stanhope has now lost the man he needed most also makes Raleigh understand how he would feel if something happened to Stanhope.

At the very end of the play, the audience is finally given a glimpse of the relationship between the two men, as Raleigh remembers it and as Stanhope wishes it could have been. Stanhope is shown to be gentle, kind and considerate, as well as heroic. His grief for Raleigh is obvious and his feelings show through even after Raleigh has died and he is briefly left alone with his thoughts. Raleigh is shown as naive and innocent, completely dependent on his friend who - no matter the personal cost - never fails him.

STANHOPE AND HIBBERT

The relationship between Stanhope and Hibbert is very different to the ones between Stanhope and Osborne or Raleigh. This is not a friendly relationship, which would stand the test of time outside of the trenches; it is much more professional and is based on the need for them to interact as two soldiers, rather than a wish, on the part of either of them, for any kind of friendship. Even from their first conversation, the audience is made awre of the tension between these two. Hibbert's first comments relate to his attempts to prove that he is not well enough to remain in the front lines and although Stanhope tries to jolly him along, Hibbert holds fast to his excuses. Only once Hibbert is out of earshot do we discover what Stanhope really thinks of him, in that he describes him to Osborne as a 'little worm'. Stanhope is determined that Hibbert will do his duty and this becomes obvious in the argument between the two men. Stanhope is initially angry about Hibbert's attitude and threatens to shoot him, but only to avoid the 'disgrace' of an inevitable court martial. It is only when Hibbert stands up to the threat made by Stanhope that the senior officer explains his own fears, eventually making Hibbert understand that he has obligations to himself and his fellow officers and then the atmosphere between them calms. Stanhope offers to help Hibbert and seems to have earned his respect.

After Osborne's death, Stanhope just wants to get drunk so that he can forget about his personal loss, while Hibbert uses the opportunity of the dinner to have a good time and show off. He goes too far with is boasting and making comments about Raleigh, which leads Stanhope to become angry and break up the party. This shows the relationship as it really is: no matter how hard Stanhope tries to tolerate and accommodate Hibbert, they will never really be able to get along. The final parting between the two men only reinforces their differences in that Stanhope is forced to get Mason to accompany Hibbert into the trenches and can barely conceal his impatience with the junior officer.

Sherriff's portrayal of this relationship serves the purpose of demonstrating more about the personalities involved, especially Hibbert as he rarely speaks to any great extent with the other characters. By Stanhope's reactions, we can appreciate how cowardly Hibbert's behaviour is, but also how the same circumstances and feelings bring out different reactions in the two men. This portrayal makes the audience more accepting and sympathetic towards Stanhope, despite his obvious problems, while it is made difficult to feel anything other than contempt for Hibbert.

Initially, after the argument over Hibbert's neuralgia, the audience might be lulled into thinking that the relationship between Stanhope and Hibbert could change into something more positive. However, the scenes at the dinner following Osborne's death reveal that deep down, nothing has changed. As far as Stanhope - and the audience - is concerned, Hibbert was a 'worm' at the beginning of the play and he is a 'worm' at the end.

TROTTER AND MASON

This is a very different relationship to all the others portrayed in the play, especially in that it is between an officer and a ranking soldier. The fact that Mason has a more familiar relationship with Trotter than with the other officers probably stems from the fact that they come from similar backgrounds. Although Trotter is an officer, he has risen through the ranks and would at the time have been classified as a 'temporary gentleman'. This status would ordinarily have made it quite difficult for him to fit in anywhere: his fellow officers might well have perceived him as being beneath them, while the ordinary soldiers could easily have felt as though he had ideas above his station. The relationships between Mason and Trotter works because they have something in common - namely food.

The conversations between these two characters demonstrate how, even in the trenches, with the tension of an impending attack, the normal, everyday things of life, such as what would be served for dinner, or why there was no pepper to go with the soup, were still important. Indeed, it could be said that these matters actually took on a greater significance at such times, not only because they served as a diversion, but also because they provided a reminder of home at a time when it must have felt very distant.

The purpose of the relationship between Trotter and Mason is to provide a domesticated element, which would help the audience to realise that the characters were really just ordinary men, placed into extraordinary circumstances. More importantly, perhaps, it also injects some humour into the play, without which it would be much less effective. Their interactions help to lighten what would otherwise be quite a dark and subdued piece, in which the only conversations would take place between officers, mainly from the same backgrounds, making the play more one dimensional. Sherriff's introduction of this relationship and the shared humour between these characters gives the whole play a different and more human emphasis.

HISTORICAL SIGNIFICANCE

The historical setting of the play is significant and accurate. The play starts on March 18th 1918 which was three days before the Germans launched "Operation Michael" at St Quentin.

This was Germany's attempt to end the war before the Americans could arrive in any great number and therefore tip the balance of power in favour of the Allies. Germany, like most of the countries involved in the First World War, was running out of men of military age and the success of this attack was therefore vital.

General Erich Ludendorff declared that the object of this attack must be a resounding victory over the British and the selection of the place for the proposed attack was therefore, of great importance. Immediately in front of the St Quentin trenches was the old Somme battlefield. This was difficult terrain which consisted of water-logged shell-holes and abandoned trenches. Ludendorff thought that, both tactically and psychologically, this was the ideal place to strike. The intention was that, by use of specialist storm troops, the German army would punch a hole in the British front line, and force a retreat towards the coast. However, Ludendorff had no fixed idea as to what would follow this initial strike.

The first days of this battle were extremely bloody and losses on both sides were heavy. It would not be surprising, therefore, if all the characters in *Journey's End* died, since the bombardment and subsequent attack resulted in many British deaths. As a result of these initial losses and the speed of the German advance, the Allied armies became separated which resulted in arguments between Haig (Commander in Chief of the British Army) and Pétain (his equivalent in the French force). At a hastily convened meeting the Allies decided to have one Supreme Commander, which it was decided should be Marshal Ferdinand Foch. This was a significant step and enabled the Allies to fight in a more co-ordinated fashion, with reserves and weaponry being better deployed.

Germany failed to exploit her initial successes and rather than continuing with the plan of a single-pronged attack, her forces became divided. In addition, the selection of the old Somme battleground now seemed unwise as it proved to be difficult terrain for an attacking army to advance over. In addition, the Germans had advanced much further than their lines of supply could support, so by 5th April the German High Command were forced to admit that Operation Michael had achieved as much as could be expected, and further attacks in this area were abandoned.

Before long, American troops began to arrive and this had a great demoralising effect on the German army. Attacks continued at other points on the front and it would take many more months, and many many more deaths before the war was over.

Field Marshal
Sir Douglas Haig

General
Henri-Philippe Pétain

Marshal
Ferdinand Foch

Photo Credits: Photo's of the Great War

The ruins of St Quentin.
Photo Credit: Photo's of the Great War

Entrance to St Quentin canal tunnel under the ridge at Bellicourt, on the Hindenburg Line.
Photo Credit: Photo's of the Great War

PORTRAYAL OF THE RANKS IN THE BRITISH ARMY

Some students find the named ranks and their responsibilities difficult to interpret. The following provides a very brief outline of the role of each of the ranks involved in *Journey's End*, together with an explanation of Sherriff's use and portrayal of these ranks.

COLONEL

The most senior officer involved in the play, the Colonel is, in all probability, in charge of a battalion of over 1000 men, divided into four companies. The company involved in *Journey's End* is 'C' Company. During the course of the war, with the influx of the New Armies and the number of casualties the quantity of men in a battalion varied widely.

In the case of *Journey's End*, the Colonel is portrayed as someone who only visits the dugout when absolutely necessary, and then only to send valuable and inexperienced men on pointless missions, while inviting Stanhope to join him for a dinner of fresh fish. Whether this portrayal was entirely intentional on Sherriff's part, is a matter of conjecture. However, many modern historians, especially those with a military background, would disagree with this heartless depiction, pointing out that if the senior officers spent all their time in the trenches, there would have been no-one left to control the overall direction of the war. Others, with more 'cultural' or 'social' agenda would argue that the senior officers were controlling the war from too great a distance, with too many perks and advantages when compared to those at the front line. Sherriff's portrayal of the Colonel would seem to indicate that he sided with the latter viewpoint, although this may be based only on his own experiences of senior officers with whom he personally came into contact. The Colonel in *Journey's End* is given few redeeming qualities. Before the raid, he speaks in a very matter-of-fact way about sending men to their possible deaths. Afterwards, he barely remembers to ask about the fate of those who went on the mission.

However, although the Colonel may seem outwardly enthusiastic, offering gushing encouragement to Raleigh and Osborne, his hesitations and embarrassed coughs show that he is also aware of the magnitude of the task at hand. One of Sherriff's reasons behind writing the play was to demonstrate the willingness of men to do their duty. The Colonel is, therefore, doing his duty, in the same way as Stanhope and all the others. He takes his orders from Brigade Headquarters and regardless of his own viewpoint, must see to it that these orders are carried out.

CAPTAIN

This rank belongs to the characters of both Stanhope and Hardy. These men are both in charge of companies of approximately 230 men. They are responsible for the maintenance of their area of trench, as well as the morale and physical well-being of the men under their command. It is their duty to ensure that the men are in a fit state to undertake whatever tasks they must perform - whether that involves fighting in battle or 'fatigues' (manual labour, such as clearing roads, digging trenches etc.)

Sherriff's portrayal of the men in this role shows that he seems to have held them in higher esteem than their superiors. This might seem hardly surprising, since this was the rank achieved by Sherriff himself! However, he was not alone in this opinion. A look at *Undertones of War* by Edmund Blunden for example, reveals a similar perspective. This memoir and Sherriff's play were both published at around the same time, and the two writers were, to a greater or lesser extent, haunted by their wartime experiences and sought to commemorate, or celebrate the comradeship and honour they had discovered during their First World War service.

In *Journey's End*, Stanhope is shown to be the man who bears all the responsibility for his men, and their well-being, while remaining extremely critical and self-effacing about his own abilities and qualities. By showing us an imperfect man, who survives on the edge, Sherriff enhances the audience's sense of sympathy for this central character. The cheerfulness of Hardy, the other Captain in the play, contrasts well with Stanhope's more troubled personality, although one should always remember that it is easier for Hardy to be cheerful as he is being relieved and going back down the line, further away from the impending attack.

LIEUTENANTS AND SECOND LIEUTENANTS

These ranks apply to all the other officers in the play. It may fairly be assumed that Osborne is superior in rank to Trotter, Hibbert and Raleigh, as he is Stanhope's second-in-command, so he probably holds the rank of Lieutenant, while the others are Second-Lieutenants. Their responsibilities were essentially to help their captain in maintaining the day-to-day running of the company. In addition, each of these men would have been responsible for a Platoon within the company, consisting of approximately 50 men each.

Sherriff portrays the few men who hold these ranks as having realistically diverse characters - from the strong, reliable Osborne, to the unpleasant, cowardly Hibbert. This reminds the audience that men from many different walks of life found themselves serving together during the First World War. There was an unprecedented mixing of classes and backgrounds in the war, which is ably depicted in the characters of Raleigh and Trotter. Raleigh is portrayed as a naive public schoolboy who has, until now, led a sheltered life, protected by his friend Stanhope, and using his family's substantial influence to achieve his ambitions. Trotter, on the other hand, would seem to be from a lower social class than Raleigh and he has been promoted through the ranks. This type of officer often found himself in a difficult position, as he did not really fit in with the 'gentleman' officers, but was equally out of place among the ordinary soldiers. While Trotter gets on quite well with all the other officers in the dugout, there is a sense of isolation within his character which may stem from a belief that he is different from them.

COMPANY SERGEANT-MAJOR

This rank is held by the most senior non-commissioned officer in a company. A commissioned officer being one who has been charged, or 'commissioned' into a specific position. The CSM is, generally speaking, responsible for standards and discipline amongst the lower ranks. Beneath him there would be other sergeants and the men. In times of battle the CSM is responsible for seeing to the safe removal of the wounded and dealing with prisoners

The CSM in *Journey's End* is an accurate representation of this rank. He oversees the German prisoner, and it is he who reports Raleigh's injuries to Stanhope and brings the wounded man into the dugout. In addition the CSM's role within the play is to remind us of the men who are out in the trenches. Being as the action takes place entirely in the dugout, the audience could easily forget the existence of anyone else without the link provided by the CSM.

Stanhope's briefing of the CSM prior to the attack also serves to further demonstrate Stanhope's character. Despite the CSM's concerns that they should have a plan for withdrawal if the enemy should overpower them, Stanhope refutes this idea. Instead, he suggests that the Company should advance, rather than retreat and should keep going until they have won the war! Stanhope is not being naive here, he is pointing out to the CSM, an experienced man himself, that they must hold their position because others are relying on them.

OTHER RANKS

These include Sergeants, Corporals, Lance Corporals and Privates. The only named 'other rank' in the play is Mason, the officer's servant, who in this role would be the only soldier, other than the officers, to spend much time in the dugout.

Although Mason is the only ranking soldier of whom we see a great deal, Sherriff portrays the unseen men as worthy of respect. Stanhope is always shown as being concerned for their welfare, checking that they have had their allocation of rum and refusing to allow an officer from another company to take part in the raid in case it damages the men's morale. Like much else in this play, this is also done to reinforce Stanhope's character. We have been told right at the beginning that Hardy had no idea where his men slept, yet Raleigh's letter demonstrates that Stanhope spends a lot of time with his men, taking great care of them.

R C SHERRIFF - BIOGRAPHY

Robert Cedric Sherriff was born on 6th June 1896 in Hampton Wick, near Kingston upon Thames in Surrey. He had an older sister, Beryl, and a younger brother, Cecil and their father, Herbert worked as an insurance clerk. Their mother, Annie Constance (née Winder) would almost certainly have met their father as a result of her family being neighbours of Herbert's brother John, when he left home, having married his wife, Bertha and moved away from the family home in Mortlake to nearby Barnes, just a few doors down from the Winder residence.

Robert was educated at Kingston Grammar School, before following his father into Sun Insurance, as a clerk on a salary of 15 shillings per week. Both his father and his grandfather had worked for this company and there had never really been any question of Robert doing anything else, although he and his father had harboured ambitions of Robert going to Oxford university, had the family's finances permitted. So, Robert settled down to a quiet, if rather dull life, commuting to the London office and working at a desk all day.

Once war was declared, Sherriff waited until after his nineteenth birthday and enlisted on November 20th 1915 in the Artists' Rifles, beginning his training at Hare Hall, Gidea Park in Essex. He wrote many letters home and was quite introspective and lonely during this time, presumably missing his family. Once his initial training was complete, Sherriff was commissioned as a Second Lieutenant and attached to the 9th Battalion of the East Surrey Regiment. He was sent for further training to Grand Shaft Barracks at Dover. From here, he embarked for France, arriving on Thursday 28th September and, within four days, had been placed in charge of a platoon of 25 men in the reserve lines, awaiting their orders to move up to the front. His first experience of front-line duty took place on 11th October, but after only four days, Sherriff's letters show that he was already beginning to feel the strain, partly due to lack of sleep. Despite this, Sherriff still found the time to appreciate his surroundings, wondering at their wrecked beauty, shattered by the repeated shelling. During the months of November and December, Sherriff was seconded to the Royal

Engineers for a tunnelling course, but upon his return, discovered that he would have to wait a further six months before being allowed any leave. He was enormously disappointed, but to pass the time, created a chart on which he could count off the passing days.

Towards the end of January 1917, Sherriff became unwell, suffering from neuralgia around his left eye and on 26th of the month, was transferred to an Officer's Rest Station behind the lines. Throughout the spring, the neuralgia returned sporadically, until he was granted a much needed ten days of leave at the end of June, returning to the trenches on 4th July. At the end of the month, he participated in the beginning of the Third Battle of Ypres, also known as Passchendaele, and a couple of days later, on 2nd August, was wounded in the face and hand, earning himself a "Blightly", so that by mid-August, he was settled in hospital at Netley in Hampshire. Although Sherriff expected to be declared fit again fairly soon, his neuralgia flared up again and he was transferred to St Thomas's Hospital in London. From there, once well, he returned to Dover, where he was employed in the training of new recruits. In March 1918, Sherriff was promoted to the rank of Lieutenant but, while waiting to be sent overseas again that summer, contracted influenza. By the time he was sufficiently recovered, the war was over, although he was promoted to the rank of Captain in January 1919.

With the war over, Sherriff returned to his job at Sun Insurance, although he gave up his desk job and went out on the road, dealing with claims and new policies, preferring the freedom that this role afforded him. To fill his spare time, Sherriff joined the nearby Kingston Rowing Club, which gave him an outlet for physical exercise, as well as the sense of belonging that he had enjoyed in the army. In 1921, the club discovered that it was in need of some new equipment and boat repairs and decided to put on an evening's entertainment in the form of sketches, musical features and a one-act play which Sherriff undertook to write. This he entitled A Hitch in the Proceedings and it was such a resounding success that the club launched the Adventurer's Dramatic Society, making their performances an annual event. Eventually they dropped the other acts and featured full three-act plays written entirely by Sherriff. This carried on for a further five years, three of which Sherriff also spent as Club captain, before he decided to give up the rowing club.

This decision meant that Sherriff found his evenings empty once again and he decided to put forward one of his rowing club plays to a London agent, selecting Curtis Brown for the purpose. He sent them his rowing club play Profit and Loss, which they liked, but rejected. He tried again, with another entitled

Cornlow on the Downs, which was once again returned. Sherriff didn't feel that his other plays were so good, and chose to turn his hand to novel writing instead. Several years earlier, he had thought up a plot based around hero-worship which featured two schoolboys: Dennis Stanhope, a popular, sporty, attractive hero; and Jimmy Raleigh, a bit of a plodder, who worships Stanhope. Upon leaving school Stanhope drifts along hopelessly, trying to live on his wits, while Raleigh does well, becoming a successful businessman. Raleigh wants to help his old schoolboy hero, but Stanhope resents every attempt that Raleigh makes. Despite having a plot outline, however, Sherriff found his own limited vocabulary a bit of an issue when it came to novel writing and before long, abandoned this idea.

As the evenings dragged on, Sherriff began to wonder whether he might be able to turn the story of Stanhope and Raleigh into a play, possibly making it more attractive to the agents by the addition of a war setting or background. Before long, this idea had taken hold and Sherriff had decided to set the entire play in a dugout, basing the characters on people he had met and the dialogue on his own experiences. It took a year to write, but when complete, Sherriff had only to find a title. He thought first of "Suspense", but rejected this as misleading; then he tried "Waiting", but thought this too commonplace. One night, while reading a book, he came upon the words: "It was late in the evening when we came at last to our Journey's End" and knew that he had found his title.

Curtis Brown responded well to the manuscript, and eventually the Incorporated Stage Society said they would put on the play on the 9th/10th December for two performances at the Apollo Theatre in London. They offered the production to a virtually known director, James Whale, and fully expected it to fail. Whale managed to procure the services of 21 year old Laurence Olivier - then an unknown actor - to play the part of Stanhope and it was agreed that all of the actors would be as little known as possible, allowing the audience to focus on the characters, rather than the men playing them. Many of the props and outfits were borrowed, with Olivier using Sherriff's uniform, which only needed the addition of an MC ribbon.

The opening performance went well, as did the second and received excellent reviews, but Sherriff's natural euphoria was short-lived: no theatre managers were interested in picking up the play. Then, on December 23rd, Sherriff was approached by Maurice Browne, who said he would produce Journey's End at the Savoy Theatre, with Whale directing. The play opened on 21st January with the same cast, except for Laurence Olivier, who had been given the lead role in Beau Geste at His Majesty's Theatre, but who was ably replaced by Colin Clive.

Again, the play was a resounding success, and ran for eighteen months, transferring to the Prince of Wales Theatre when the Savoy closed for refurbishment. It was translated into 27 languages and performed around the world, enabling Sherriff to eventually relinquish his job at Sun Insurance. His new-found fame brought him into contact with other literary notables, including H. G. Wells, Somerset Maugham, Ivor Novello, Rebecca West and, eventually two of his greatest heroes, Rudyard Kipling and J. M. Barrie. In 1930, the play was made into a film in Hollywood with James Whale directing, but back in England, people were clamouring for Sherriff's next play. After a few false starts, he wrote a story of English village life, entitled Badger's Green, which failed dismally to entice either critics or audiences.

This failure caused Sherriff a few financial problems. While Journey's End was at the height of its success, he had earned well and had bought a house at Esher in Surrey called Rosebriars. Once furnished, the total cost of this purchase came to around £10,000 and he needed an income of approximately £5,000 per year to maintain the property, but once Journey's End closed, and Badger's Green failed, he was only earning about one quarter of this. He needed another success. With his capital dwindling, Sherriff decided to enrol at university, with a view to becoming a schoolmaster. After one unsuccessful interview, Sherriff was accepted, in 1931, at New College, Oxford and that summer, while waiting to go up, decided to write a novel, entitled The Fortnight in September, which met with great critical acclaim and sold in tens of thousands.

In Autumn 1931, Sherriff rented a small house in Oxford, which he shared with his mother, and began his studies in history. He also rekindled his keen interest in rowing, having been a member of the Leander Club, and was welcomed with open arms by the college eight, rowing at number 7. At the end of the season, the captain informed Sherriff that he would be recommending him the following year for a place in the University crew: Sherriff, at the age of 36 would have the opportunity to earn a coveted Oxford Blue.

In the spring of 1932, Sherriff received a surprise letter from James Whale, who was now working for Universal Pictures in Hollywood, inviting Sherriff to go to America to write the screenplay for The Invisible Man by H. G. Wells. Although Sherriff was very tempted by this kind and lucrative offer, he also still felt drawn to Oxford and the chance of his Blue, as well as acknowledging his indebtedness to the warden of New College for allowing him to study there as a Special Student in the first place. The warden came to his rescue, suggesting that Sherriff take an elongated summer break, go to Hollywood and return to Oxford the following autumn.

So, in spring 1932, Sherriff and his mother travelled to Hollywood, where he worked diligently on the screenplay, avoided the loud, late-night parties, but enjoyed quiet and entertaining dinners with Charlie Chaplin, Ronald Colman, Boris Karloff and Norma Shearer among many others. When the job was done, Universal offered him a very profitable contract to stay on in Hollywood, which he declined, recalling not only his promise to the warden, but also the coveted Oxford Blue that might still be his. Sherriff and his mother returned to England, arriving in Liverpool on August 12th 1932.

Autumn saw Sherriff back on the river, practising hard to get back into shape. He did well, getting through the first two trials, before becoming ill. He was diagnosed with pleurisy and ordered to rest. Sherriff's disappointment was complete when he was later informed that he would definitely have been selected for the Oxford crew, had his health not failed him. More bad news followed, in a meeting between Sherriff and his tutor, in which the latter pointed out that Sherriff would be lucky to scrape a pass and might even fail his degree, but would certainly not achieve the honours required to become a schoolmaster. Sherriff was philosophical in his disappointment: he had gained a great deal from his Oxford experience and would always be grateful for the opportunity. He was only half-sad, therefore, to pick up his pen and write to Universal Pictures, who had left their offer open, suggesting in doing so, that he could work from home, rather than in Hollywood.

Writing in England and sending the scripts to America was more difficult than Sherriff had imagined and, after two failed screenplays, he and Universal parted company. Sherriff began to worry that he'd taken a wrong turn in leaving Oxford, when he was approached by studio owner Alexander Korda, who was building his own facility at Denham in Buckinghamshire. He wanted Sherriff to write the screenplay for The Four Feathers by A E W Mason, which proved to be another resounding success. This was followed by Goodbye Mr Chips, written for MGM, for which Sherriff was Oscar-nominated.

Despite his movie successes, Sherriff longed to return to his first-love in the theatre and, with actress Jeanne de Casalis wrote St Helena, based on the final day of Napolean Bonaparte. After a faltering start, this turned into another success at the Old Vic. Sherriff, now financially more secure, spent the next three years from 1936 to 1939 setting up and funding an archaeological dig at Angmering in Sussex, where the remains of a Roman villa had been discovered. He found this a thoroughly enjoyable and rewarding experience, brought to an end only by the beginning of the Second World War.

Initially, Sherriff was employed by the Ministry of Information to write propaganda and also to help recruit people into joining the A.R.P. Then in spring 1940, Korda contacted him again, wanting another screenplay - this time for Lady Hamilton (also known as That Hamilton Woman). After a very difficult journey, Sherriff and his mother arrived in Hollywood, where he was pleased to renew his acquaintance with Laurence Olivier who was going to star in the film, alongside his new wife, Vivien Leigh. Once production was complete, Sherriff worked on Mrs Miniver and then This Above All. He wanted to return to England, but it was impossible to secure a passage without a good reason, so Korda provided him with a contract that required him to be in London. Just as Sherriff and his mother were about to depart, the Japanese attacked Pearl Harbour, throwing everyone on the West coast into a state of panic. They had to wait for a safe passage and didn't end up returning to England until 7th August 1944 on board the Cunard ship Rangitata.

After the war, Sherriff began to tire of screenwriting and, after a fifteen year gap, decided to write another play. This was the story of a kindly, poor spinster who murders her wealthy mean, widowed sister, so that she can pass her money onto worthy causes. Sherriff entitled the play Miss Mable and it went on at The Duchess Theatre becoming a triumph, and running for six months. Thus inspired, Sherriff wrote Home at Seven, which was performed at The Wyndham's Theatre with Ralph Richardson in the lead role. He scored another hit, the play running for 342 performances in the West End.

Sherriff then wrote a play called The Long Sunset, in the mid 1950s. The inspiration for this came from his time at Angmering excavating the Roman villa and told the story of a Roman family living in Britain. He offered the play to the BBC for their Saturday Night Theatre slot, through which it reached a radio audience of around five million listeners. It was then performed at the Birmingham Repertory Theatre and Bernard Miles put it on at the Mermaid Theatre in London. The Cambridge examining board chose the text as the Modern English play for their English examination that year. Schools flocked to the theatre and Sherriff gave talks prior to the performances.

Then, quite unexpectedly Hollywood resurfaced, offering Sherriff something that he considered as "the best": the screenplay for The Dambusters. With this under his belt, the world was his oyster and he wrote further novels, plays and screenplays until the theatre became too modern and readers tired of his style of writing: there were younger - but not necessarily better - men to fill his shoes, and he reluctantly passed the baton to them.

Sherriff lived quietly at Rosebriars in Esher until his death on 13th November 1975. He bequeathed his house to Elmbridge Borough Council for social and cultural purposes and the money raised from the sale of the property established the R C Sherriff Rosebriars Trust which still exists today, promoting and assisting the arts in the Borough of Elmbridge.

PERFORMANCE FEATURES

In looking at performance techniques, students can examine not only the intention of the original playwright, but also how the play is adapted and interpreted by other directors. The playwright's ideas or instructions are usually written down within the script and, in the case of *Journey's End*, Sherriff has been quite precise as to how and where everything should be positioned and the movement and actions of the characters.

When looking at the interpretations of more modern directors, this can only be done when a performance of the play has actually been seen, which is not always possible. I was able to see a production of *Journey's End* in 2008, which was, in many ways, quite different to the one envisaged by Sherriff. However, this enables me to, hopefully, provide some useful insight for students.

SETTING

Journey's End is set entirely in a dugout during the few days prior to the German Spring Offensive which began on 21st March 1918. In the play, Sherriff gave specific instructions as to how the dugout should look, including the layout and style of the furniture and the 'magazine pictures pinned to the wall of girls in flimsy costumes'. His own experiences provided him with the background knowledge to make this setting as realistic as possible and thus create the required tension needed within this confined space. The presence of the war is really quite remote to the audience, who in the original play only heard its sounds 'faint and far away'.

In a modern version of the play, the director would normally adhere to broadly these same guidelines, although they could, of course, move things around somewhat. The other differences could include the use of projections above or behind the dugout scene to give the audience an idea of what is taking place in the trenches.

LIGHTING

Sherriff's directions include lighting from the outside in the form of moonlight and Very lights, as well as a 'pale shaft of sunlight' in the morning scenes. Within the dugout, there are candles on the table. In this way, the impression can be created that anyone not seated at the table is in semi-darkness. With the use of theatre lights, this element can be enhanced to suit the mood of particular scenes.

In a modern production, it is significantly easier to make use of lighting effects, which may be employed to generate an atmosphere of tension or high emotion. A perfect example of this could be the scene when Raleigh dies in which only that area of the stage is lit, while the remainder is left in comparative darkness. Once Raleigh has died and Stanhope is alone, the director then focuses a single light on him, leaving Raleigh in subdued shadow, so the audience know that he is still there, but are concentrating on Stanhope's expressions and reactions.

SOUND EFFECTS

Being as the audience of the original production could never actually see anything to do with the action of the war, the sound effects were very important in creating an authentic atmosphere. This is especially the case during the raid, when nothing is actually happening on the stage. Everything is left to the audience's imagination at this point and given the events that are to follow, it is important that the raid should sound as dramatic as possible.

More modern productions can take advantage of different forms of sound effects and mindle these with visual and graphic elements to create something more dramatic, but probably less realistic. Music can also be used, although this is not always appropriate and can sometimes detract from the audience's concentration on a specific moment in the play.

NON-VERBAL COMMUNICATIONS

Regardless of when the play is produced, the power and quality of the non-verbal communications is of vital importance. These will quite often take the form of looks, glances and meaningful silences between two or more characters and can, if handled well by both directors and actors, speak volumes. There are moments where 'eyes meet' between two characters, most notably at the time when Stanhope and Osborne part company and when Osborne and Raleigh are about to go on the raid. These small devices create an emotional link between the characters which words could not have done, mainly because in such as situation, these men would have shied away from saying what they really felt, but could express it with one simple look.

COSTUMES AND PROPS

In the original production, most of the costumes and props were either improvised or borrowed. So, for example, Laurence Olivier, as Stanhope, wore Sherriff's army uniform. Sherriff had been a captain in the war, so the only addition needed was an MC ribbon to make it perfect for Stanhope.

Modern productions often make use of purpose-made, rather than original, uniforms and props, which are perfectly adequate from the perspective of the audience. Occasionally a director may choose to inject a little modernity into the production, but in the case of *Journey's End*, this rarely works.

ENDING

According to the directions given, the play ends with Stanhope leaving the dugout and, as a shell lands nearby, the 'timber props of the roof cave slowly in'. The stage is in darkness with only the occasional light of the coming dawn showing through the cracks of the 'broken doorway'. In the distance, machine-gun and rifle fire can be heard. Being as no other directions are given, we may assume that at this point, the curtain fell.

The ending of the play is something with which modern directors have been able to meddle. While the departure of Stanhope must, essentially, remain the same, directors are free to change what happens next. Some miss out the destruction of the dugout, drop the curtain and project a poignant scene, such as poppies. Others simply leave the stage in darkness. In the production which I saw, the ending was especially well handled. After Stanhope had mounted the steps and the gunfire had ceased, the Last Post was sounded. The stage was darkened and the cast marched out to stand in a dim light at the front of the stage in one line, facing the audience. At this point, the audience began to applaud. Then the actor playing the Company Sergeant Major stepped forward and, in a voice raised above the applause, gave the order to salute, before dismissing the Company. They didn't bow, or even acknowledge the audience, but remained in character and it really felt as though they were saluting and individually paying tribute to the men they had been portraying.

THEMES

FUTILITY AND WASTE

Journey's End is now generally recognised as an anti-war play, although some historians doubt that this was Sherriff's original intention. Some confusion, it would seem, arose from a difference of opinion between Sherriff and the play's original producer. Sherriff's intention was, rather, to portray the pride which the men felt in each other and the comradeships which developed in such difficult circumstances. In doing so, he also demonstrates the inescapable human cost of the war. The men seem to be required to make great sacrifices and it is made clear that even those who survived would never be the same again. Death is indiscriminate, taking those who least deserve to fall, and these deaths are seen to serve little or no purpose. Any gains made are certainly not worth the loss of such valued characters. The men are generally portrayed as worthy people who have accepted their presence in the war as a duty they have to perform - a necessary evil. Although the men, especially Stanhope, may question the value of activities such as the raid, none of them speak out against the war itself, despite the fact that it costs them all dearly.

These themes are best demonstrated immediately before and after the raid, led by Osborne and Raleigh. The purpose of this raid is to capture some German soldiers to find out where the anticipated attack is likely to take place, and the strength and nature of the opposing army. The colonel points out, somewhat optimistically, that the success of this raid may constitute an Allied victory. However, the discovery of the type of opposition you are facing is unlikely to affect the outcome of a battle, if you have nothing more to throw at it yourself. Therefore, it would seem that the colonel is seeking to justify the raid, when in fact, as Stanhope suggests, there can be no justification for such a waste of lives. The raiding party manages to capture a young German soldier, whose limited information is greeted with disproportionate pleasure by the Colonel. He appears to feel that the raid has accomplished its aims. The details given by the captured German soldier, however, seem insignificant compared with the loss of life necessitated during his seizure.

The deaths of Osborne and six of the men accompanying him, is a great price for this Company to pay. For Osborne - surely the most likeable character in the play - to have died at all is lamentable, but to have died for so little and in such circumstances is tragic - a point which Stanhope grasps, and which makes him bitter and angry towards the Colonel. Stanhope appreciates that it is really Osborne who holds the Company together, not himself, because he has come to rely so heavily on Osborne as the war has progressed. Nothing has really been gained by these deaths and Sherriff uses Osborne's death in particular to reinforce the idea of this war's wanton destruction of the best men of his generation.

Throughout the play, however, Sherriff also shows that death is not the only means of wasting a life: Stanhope has virtually suffered a nervous breakdown, changing from the self-assured, sportsman and hero of Raleigh's description, to a confused and moody wreck, who doubts his own abilities and constantly looks to Osborne for reassurance. Raleigh, on the other hand, loses his innocence: he learns a difficult lesson as he comes to realise that Stanhope is not the man he once knew and that the war has changed his friend forever. Ultimately Raleigh also loses his life - within a few minutes of his first experience of battle - but not before he has witnessed the physical and emotional damage that the war can bring about. Had either Stanhope or Raleigh lived, it is unlikely that they would ever have fully recovered from their experiences. Stanhope actually realises this already, as he shows in his conversation with Osborne, when he says that if he survives he will go away by himself for a long time, to recover his health, before trying to face Madge again.

Another example of futility comes in a seemingly strange conversation when Osborne and Stanhope discuss the fate of worms. The two men agree that worms probably have no idea in which direction they are travelling and how rotten and confusing this must be for them. This minor conversation could be interpreted as a reference to the equal pointlessness of the men's existence - they also have very little idea of where they are going, or why, and yet as Osborne says - with more than an air of sarcasm, this pointlessness and confusion is dreaded by the worms more than anything else. He is implying that there are worse situations to be in than wasting your time drifting aimlessly; being killed, without ever really understanding the reason, for example, could as easily befall the worm or the soldier.

The choice of *Alice's Adventures in Wonderland* as reading material for Osborne is also interesting. Osborne quotes from the book to Trotter, who finds the passage pointless and playfully mocks Osborne for reading a children's book. Of course,

Osborne's point is that it *is* pointless - not just the passage quoted, but everything - this story represents how little meaning there is in the men's lives, and how nonsensical the whole war has become. For most of the men, especially those like Stanhope and Raleigh, the point of joining up was for the "adventure" and to do their duty, not to sit around in trenches, waiting to be blown up, or being sent on pointless raids into No Man's Land.

BOREDOM AND TENSION

Most of the play is spent waiting for something to happen, whether it is a raid, the impending attack or the serving of a meal. Hardy tells us right at the beginning of the play that the men can sit in boredom for hours and hours and then, suddenly, without warning, something unexpected will happen.

The tension created by this sense of anticipation provokes different responses in each of the characters. Hibbert, for example, dreads going up into the trenches and longs for the waiting to continue - anything as long as he doesn't have to face the realities of his situation. He spends most of his time asleep in his dugout, not mixing with the other men. By avoiding them he also avoids the issue of what might be about to happen, because he is not there to hear it being discussed. His supposed illness is his means of trying to escape, although it also tells us a lot about his personality. Hibbert's reaction is a form of denial: by pretending to be unwell and avoiding the others, he is trying to appear as though the war has not really affected him psychologically, but that it has made him physically ill. The truth, of course, is revealed during his argument with Stanhope, when he is forced to confess his real feelings.

Stanhope on the other hand, 'copes' by keeping busy, not sleeping and drinking himself into oblivion. By doing this he not only takes his mind off the reality of his life, but also helps to pass the time doing anything other than thinking - a necessity of his position which has become abhorrent to him. In addition to not thinking about his current situation any more than is absolutely necessary, Stanhope also seems to have been avoiding thoughts of his past. Raleigh's arrival necessities a resurgence of these memories and, for the first time, he tells Osborne about his feelings for Madge. Osborne is Stanhope's closest friend and yet he has never spoken of Raleigh's sister before. He has obviously found it necessary to block out his memories of the past, in order to maintain a semblance of a focus on the present. Remembering these things only seems to add to his tensions which become more obvious as the raid approaches. He paces the floor, glances about anxiously, checks his watch repeatedly - showing that the strain of waiting is making him even more nervous than normal. He also busies himself with the last-minute preparations so as to avoid thinking about what might happen.

Osborne tries to help wherever he can and relieves his boredom by reading *Alice's Adventures in Wonderland*. He is a great observer of everything which is happening around him. He talks to the others, helping to relieve their nerves, especially Raleigh, who has no idea what to expect. Probably the most tense moment in the play is the scene between Raleigh and Osborne immediately prior to the raid. Once they have finalised their plans, Osborne suggests that they try to forget about the raid for the final few minutes before it commences. It takes several attempts and a quotation from *Alice in Wonderland* before Osborne succeeds in changing the subject. The tension actually seems to increase as they discuss their homes and talk of Osborne visiting Raleigh after the war. There is an unspoken fear that, in all probability, one or other of these men may not return and they make plans for the future to cover this up.

Trotter eats, thinks about eating, or talks about eating, and writes to his wife of mundane, everyday matters, such as his garden and the lice which have infested his clothing. He has created a chart of circles to count down the hours until they can be relieved and go back down the line. Trotter uses humour to overcome these difficult situations, although there is always the underlying hint that he feels much more than he expresses.

Only Raleigh, the new recruit is, as yet, unaffected by the boredom, as he is keen to impress the others and everything is a new experience for him, so he pays attention and makes sure that he is doing his duty to the best of his ability. Although he is unaware of what lies ahead in the raid, the tension of waiting to go out into No Man's Land is obvious and his nerves start to get the better of his excitement, although Osborne helps to calm him down. Once Osborne has been killed, Raleigh's sense of adventure and excited anticipation disappear, to be replaced by the same sense of sorrow and foreboding as the rest of the men.

In reality these feelings of boredom and tension were common among serving soldiers in the First World War. Much of a soldier's time was spent carrying out fatigues, waiting behind the lines in reserve to be called back to the front. The pent up anticipation and fear which accumulated as they waited for the inevitable attack is admirably captured in this play. The feelings of terror during battles could be said to have been increased by the fact that so much of their time was spent doing mundane and repetitive tasks, waiting for something to happen. It was all or nothing.

SCHOOLDAYS AND HEROES

There is a strong link in this play between life in the trenches and at a "public" school. Not only were Raleigh and Stanhope at the same school, but Osborne, in private life, was a schoolmaster. At the time of the First World War, the title "public" school was given to fee-paying establishments, of which many were also boarding schools. There is an atmosphere of the school dormitory in the dugout, and a definite sense of hierarchy, with certain officers taking precedence over others, and the emphasis being on experience and seniority. For instance, right at the beginning of the play, Hardy points out the best bed in the dugout to Osborne, telling him that the others do not have bottoms to them. As the senior officer of his Company, Hardy has the best bed, while the other officers have to make do with whatever is left. Interestingly though, Stanhope designates the best bed to Osborne, preferring to sleep nearer to the table, so he can work during the night without disturbing anyone else.

Stanhope is given the air of the "head boy", looking after those younger or less experienced than himself, especially the new boy - Raleigh. Although we are led to believe that Stanhope was happy to wear this mantle while at school, it does not sit so well with him now. He says that he used to enjoy looking after Raleigh and the influence that he was able to exert over the younger boy, but now he feels uncomfortable at having so much additional responsibility thrust upon him. He also wishes that he could have been spared the indignity of having Raleigh witness what has become of him - he feels that his hero's crown has slipped and does not want to crush Raleigh's image of him. It would seem that Stanhope took his status at school quite seriously. Raleigh recalls Stanhope's attitude towards smoking and drinking when they were at school, which goes to show how much of an impact the war has had, being as Stanhope now drinks so much himself.

Raleigh, on the other hand, as the new boy is eager to please and do well, just as he probably would have been at school. His personality makes him keen to learn, although he is as yet unsure of the rules and protocols which exist in the trenches. At school, Raleigh had worshiped Stanhope and looked up to him as someone worthy of respect, finding it impossible to see a fault in Stanhope's personality. He is keen that this relationship should continue in the trenches and hopes that Stanhope will not object to his presence. Osborne has to try and warn Raleigh about his hero's altered personality and the effect that the war has had on him. Raleigh's hopes for a resumption of his friendship with Stanhope may be because he assumes that the continuation of certain aspects of his life at home will give him an increased sense of security - reminding him, perhaps, of happier days at school.

Osborne, with his worldly experience is the voice of reason and sanity - the housemaster. He offers sensible advice and provides a caring, responsible figure for the others to turn to. As a former schoolmaster, himself he is perfectly suited to this role as he understands the problems of boys who find themselves away from home, thrust into unfamiliar territory. It must be remembered that Stanhope, when he first went out to the front, and Raleigh, when he arrives, are extremely young - and have arrived straight from school. Osborne's presence must be very welcome and reassuring to both of them, especially given Stanhope's instability. A good example of this relationship is when Stanhope asks Osborne to tuck him up in bed - this shows not only Stanhope's youth, but also Osborne's caring and understanding nature.

We also have Mason, who in the role of servant, helps recreate the public school hierarchy. Many of the boys in a public school at that time would have been accustomed to having servants at home, and within the school itself, younger boys were often expected to fetch and carry (or 'fag') for the more senior pupils. The officers chastise Mason for not bringing any pepper to go with their soup, and he worries (quite disproportionately) about the prospect of having to serve apricots instead of the desired pineapple. His worries serve to remind us of his 'inferior' status, when compared to the officers and also of how important mundane matters, such as food, have become to the men.

Trotter is the only one of the officers who, it would seem, did not attend a public school. This is demonstrated by his tone and language, which is more colloquial than the others. Also, we learn that he has risen from the ranks which is interesting, as it means that rather than being commissioned as an officer from the very beginning, he has worked his way up, by being good at what he does. The difference in his education could provide a reason why Trotter keeps his views to himself most of the time: although they are all friendly enough, he possibly does not feel that he really fits in with the others.

Stanhope's treatment of Hibbert, when the latter tries to evade his duties, is equally reminiscent of schooldays. Although he is obviously more extreme in his language and the nature of his threats, one can easily imagine Stanhope berating Hibbert for refusing to turn out for a rugby match, or not doing his best in the last game of cricket. Hibbert is, in fact, the only member of the company who does not show Stanhope very much respect, but then we are not told what his background is, so we do not know whether he was a public schoolboy. His language ties in with most of the other officers, but his behaviour is not so honourable as theirs. It is possible, therefore, that Hibbert's education was of a 'grammar school' nature. Grammar schools at this time would have also been fee-paying, but the charges would have been much smaller than those of 'public' schools and provided a sound education. Hibbert's less than appealing character could be the result of his belief that he has had less opportunities in life than his public school comrades, for whom he may have harboured some resentment.

Within the play there are also many references to rugby and cricket which help reinforce this 'public school' image of England as it was before the First World War when those sports would have been standard and duty and loyalty to the team and one's friends would have been implicit. To be chosen to play for the team was an honour, although such a selection also had the effect of creating heroes, since those chosen were often lauded by their contemporaries, in the same way as top footballers are today.

THE EFFECTS OF WAR ON THE INDIVIDUAL

This is a common theme within the literature of the First World War and it is not surprising that it features in *Journey's End*, bearing in mind Sherriff's first-hand experiences of the conflict. As well as undergoing some changes himself, he would also have witnessed the ways in which the war affected everyone around him.

As a play, rather than a novel, *Journey's End* provides a different opportunity for examining the concept of how war might affect an individual. Rather than relying on language and literary devices, Sherriff had the advantage of being able to use expression and physical actions to portray this element. In this way, for example, Stanhope's dependence on alcohol is more poignant because the actor can portray, with a look at the bottle or a pause over the glass, how much he needs that next drink. Equally, the deaths of Osborne and Raleigh are not only brought more vividly to life, but so is Stanhope's reaction, in that the audience can see his grief on his face and hear it in his voice.

The most obvious character who Sherriff wants the audience to see as being changed by his war experiences, is Stanhope and this is made clear from his very first appearance. The audience has already been made aware by Raleigh that he and Stanhope attended school together and we have also been told that Raleigh is a 'well-built, healthy-looking boy of about eighteen, with the new uniform of a second lieutenant.' A little later, when Stanhope enters the dugout, his description is a little different, but in quite subtle ways. We are informed at once that he is 'no more than a boy' and that he takes care of his appearance, making him seem, at first glance, quite similar to Raleigh. Then, however, Sherriff points out his 'old and war-stained' uniform and the 'pallor under his skin' which, coupled with the 'dark shadows under his eyes' give away the length of time he has spent in the trenches and his exhaustion. The difference between the two men, as well as their similarities in age, helps the audience to immediately see the impact that being in the trenches has had on Stanhope.

This aspect is reinforced by Raleigh's descriptions of his time at school with Stanhope, which can then be contrasted with Stanhope's actual behaviour within the play, which the audience can witness at first hand. This is probably most obvious in the scene centred around Raleigh's letter. The disparity between the actual content of Raleigh's letter and Stanhope's violent reaction to him is so marked that it leaves the audience in no doubt as to Stanhope's state of mind. This, coupled with Raleigh's response to Stanhope at the time, which borders on fear, allows us to really see the changes in him through the eyes, not only of someone who really knows him, but also of someone who is still an innocent.

Stanhope is the most obviously war-weary character in the play. He has the shortest temper and is prone to flaring up at the slighted provocation, partly because he is always tired or drunk and partly because the responsibility for all the men around him has fallen on his shoulders. We learn that taking responsibility for others is not a new concept for Stanhope, but during war, those responsibilities are significantly heightened. They no longer relate to school or sports activities, but to life and death. This has clearly come to weigh heavily on Stanhope as time has progressed.

In order to see how the war impacts on Stanhope, we can also look at how it affects his old friend Raleigh and how their relationship changes. At the beginning of the play, Raleigh shows a keen innocence for what lies ahead. The audience is aware of his naiveté because of the conversation that has taken place between Osborne and Hardy, which has revealed a little about Stanhope and something of the realities of the war. Raleigh retains this innocence until after the incident regarding his letter, at which point he becomes a little more guarded around Stanhope, although he is still excited when he is chosen to accompany Osborne on the raid. It is only after Osborne's death that we can really perceive any change in Raleigh and that is brought about by Stanhope's altered attitude to him. Raleigh is confused by Stanhope's reaction to the loss of Osborne, interpreting the dinner as a celebration, rather than a means of forgetting. Again, this really shows the inexperience of Raleigh and it angers Stanhope that his friend has failed to comprehend the situation. The realisation of how much Stanhope cared for Osborne hits Raleigh quite hard, mainly because he doesn't know how to react anymore. His friendship with Stanhope has altered and there is too much distance between them now for him to cross back.

Although the war has an enormous impact on Stanhope's character, it is fair to say that the greatest alterations which the audience witnesses are caused by death, rather than the actual conflict. Firstly, following Osborne's death, Stanhope is initially humorous and hearty, trying to hide from the pain of his loss. Then he turns his anger and grief onto Raleigh, who probably respects him more than anyone else. Finally, when Raleigh dies, the audience sees a true transformation in a character, as Stanhope cares, with a remarkable intensity and compassion, for his dying friend. In this way, Sherriff gives his audience hope, showing us that, no matter how bad the damage, the man himself always had a chance of redemption and was never completely lost.

FAMILY

Whilst these men are all very different, in terms of background, experience and personality, they have become like a family and have adopted roles within that family. There is a powerful sense of belonging and of loyalty which most of the men exhibit throughout the play and those who do not are chastised for their attitude.

Osborne, the oldest and wisest, is nicknamed "Uncle" - a well deserved and appropriate epithet since he is always on hand with sensible advice, is supremely loyal and kind, yet not overbearing or interfering. His maturity and experience, both before and during the war, help him to understand the others. Osborne's adoption of this nickname enhances this family theme and encourages the audience or reader to look for further examples of it.

Stanhope, despite his youth, is a father-figure to his men - which was not an uncommon role for company commanders in the First World War. He has to take all the tough decisions and deal with the consequences both of his own and others' actions. This responsibility weighs heavily on one so young, and has taken its toll on Stanhope, who is on the verge of a nervous breakdown relying heavily on the senior members of his "family" for support. Their loyalty and respect for him are obvious - and well deserved. Despite his many faults, he always puts them first.

Raleigh is the equivalent of the youngest son in the family - looking to his elders for advice and approval. He worships Stanhope blindly and his attachment to his friend is clear: when writing to his family at home, he makes no mention of Stanhope's problems with alcohol or his changed temperament - putting any noticeable changes in Stanhope's personality down to tiredness and overwork. Like many younger sons, he doesn't yet have a fixed idea of what his future holds and is content, for the time being, at least, to follow in the footsteps of those who have preceded him.

The role of older brother goes to Trotter, who is quiet, considerate and has a good sense of humour which sees the family through difficult times. He keeps his own counsel and doesn't interfere but is willing to help when asked. Again, he is loyal to Stanhope, but in a less obvious, more considered manner. He is not blind to Stanhope's faults, but understands their cause and his age and experience allow him to be more tolerant of his surroundings and of the behaviour of others.

Hibbert is the "Black Sheep" of the family, and he sometimes embarrasses those around him by his comments and outbursts. He is the only selfish member of the "family", and his loyalties lie entirely with himself. He shows little or no respect for Stanhope or his fellow officers and his main concern is how to avoid any further involvement in the war.

Mason, in his role as cook, is the equivalent of the household servant, tending to the needs of the family. His loyalty is to all of them, but he answers mainly to Stanhope, who is perceived as the head of the house.

HUMOUR

There is a very effective use of humour, usually of a 'gallows' style, throughout the play. Very early on, during Hardy's conversation with Osborne, the use of humour demonstrates the need for relief from the everyday horrors of war. The number of rats, the condition of the dugout and beds, the poor storage of ammunition, all of which are very important, are treated in a flippant, lighthearted manner. Other matters, too are treated in the same way, for example the lack of pepper to go with the officer's soup brings a wry comment from Trotter, whose interest in food provides the source of several other jokes. The fact that important and insignificant issues are treated in the same manner shows that, even things which in peacetime might seem unimportant, can, at times of extreme stress, take on a completely different emphasis.

Much of the humour in the play centres around Mason, the cook/servant. His witty responses regarding his cooking, the quality of the food that he is supplying or his standards of hygiene give the play a more homely quality and help to relieve the continually building tension. It should be born in mind that the original audience of the play would have been aware of the significance of the dates during which the action takes place and would have understood the consequences of setting the play at this time. It would have been essential for the author to lighten and relieve the audience's perception of the situation in which the men found themselves. An audience must be entertained as well as enlightened, otherwise the play could never hope to succeed.

This use of humour also helps define the surroundings and the men's state of mind. This could probably have been achieved without the humour, but it would have been less effective. The realistic use of humour makes the whole situation more human, which in turn draws the audience into the world of these men, forcing us to care even more about their survival. We can also appreciate their capacity, through humour, to triumph in the face of adversity - to not give in to their fears and apprehensions, but to rise above them.

Sherriff's use of humour is, at times, more subtle - for example near the end of the play, just before the attack, when Trotter is singing in his dugout, Stanhope throws him a few coins, as though he were a street performer, and Trotter replies in kind. This humour helps in the creation of the atmosphere of camaraderie which is what has kept the men going in the dugout. This is reflected in many of the memoirs written by soldiers who served during the First World War. Without being able to crack a joke, or have a laugh, the tension would have been almost unbearable.

COMPARISONS

Within the realms of A-level studies, it is often required of students that they compare and contrast one piece of literature with another, which naturally requires a far greater level of understanding of both pieces and can also necessitate wider reading. Making such comparisons is good practice for students, forcing them into the habit of reading as widely as possible, from as many different sources as are available. This helps with the interpretation and understanding of literature, as well as enabling the student to have a broader perspective of the time during which a piece was written, and how this can influence the writing. The following provides a series of topics contained in *Journey's End* which could be compared or contrasted with other literature of the First World War, including other plays, novels and poems.

MALE RELATIONSHIPS

The first important point to note, within this topic, is the time of publication. *Journey's End* was first published in 1929, which would have made an openly homosexual relationship between two characters impossible, being as homosexuality was, at that time, illegal. This also applies to other books published at that time, such as Remarque's *All Quiet on the Western Front* (1929) and Rebecca West's *The Return of the Soldier* (1918). Novels which have been published in the second half of the twentieth century such as Susan Hill's *Strange Meeting* (1971), Pat Barker's *Regeneration* (1991) and Sebastian Faulks' *Birdsong* (1993) do not have this restriction and the modern authors are therefore able to be more explicit in their content and language, if they choose.However, this difference in the date of publication does not necessarily mean that the more modern authors always refer to this type of relationship between their male characters.

In *Journey's End* the main relationship explored by students is usually that between Stanhope and Raleigh. Stanhope is the senior officer and Raleigh is the new recruit, determined to do well. These two men knew each other before the war and, in fact, Stanhope has "an understanding" with Raleigh's sister. They attended the same school and, Stanhope being good at sport, became an object of hero-worship to Raleigh, and probably many of the other boys at school, even before the war. This has been enhanced by his long service in the trenches, the award of an MC and his command of a Company. Raleigh's feelings for Stanhope could be said to border on a schoolboy "crush", although that is open to interpretation and his somewhat gushing descriptions of Stanhope could be put down to his youthful enthusiasm. He clearly looks up to his friend, while Stanhope feels under great pressure to protect the younger man - an almost impossible task, given their current surroundings. Stanhope's reactions to Raleigh are also tempered by his fear that Raleigh will inform his family, and therefore his sister, of the effect that the war has had on Stanhope's personality. The impression created is that Stanhope has always been popular with Raleigh's family and he is terrified of losing their respect. He has, in fact, managed to avoid seeing either his or Raleigh's family for some time - he would prefer them all to remember him how he was and he can cope better knowing that they continue to believe in him. There is no hint of homosexual love between these two men - in fact Raleigh seems to feel quite honoured that there is a budding romance between his sister and Stanhope.

Sherriff uses the relationship between Stanhope and Raleigh for many purposes: to demonstrate the destructive nature of the war on a man's personality; to highlight the loss of innocence in many young men as a result of their experiences in the trenches; to show the audience how a 'flawed' character like Stanhope can still inspire hero-worship, despite his perceived faults. Raleigh never really loses his faith in Stanhope, and eventually rewarded on his death-bed with a glimpse of his old hero.

Another equally important relationship in *Journey's End* is the one between Stanhope and Osborne. Here, although he is the junior officer, it is really Osborne who is portrayed as the stronger character of the two. His knowledge and understanding of Stanhope enable him to sympathise with his Commanding Officer. He still does his duty while protecting Stanhope from his own self-destruction. Stanhope is occasionally portrayed as almost childlike, which gives his relationship with Osborne a father-and-son perspective. If anything, one feels that the roles should be reversed and that Osborne should be in charge - but like much else in this portrayal of the war - things are not always as they should be. Osborne unashamedly declares his love for Stanhope right at the beginning of the play, but the audience is under no misapprehension that this is a romantic love. He is stating a depth of feeling which shows how much Stanhope means to him - he would willingly follow Stanhope to Hell - but this is due to Osborne's

unlimited respect for him, coupled with a mutual understanding and
compassion. Sherriff's portrayal of this relationship helps to demonstrate
Stanhope's comparative youth and contrasts it with the responsibilities he now
has to bear. In addition, Sherriff makes the audience compare this relationship
with Stanhope's treatment of Raleigh.

Within this theme, the relationship between Siegfried Sassoon and Wilfred
Owen as portrayed in Pat Barker's *Regeneration*, bears some scrutiny. This can,
however, be complicated by the fact that there also existed a real-life friendship
between them and that *Regeneration* is the first part of a trilogy, so their story is,
at the end of this novel, incomplete. Owen hero-worships Sassoon - after all he
has shown himself to be a courageous officer, renowned for his daring exploits at
the front and is, of course, a published poet - something of which Owen, at this
stage, can only dream. Like Raleigh, Owen is always prepared to excuse any sign
of rudeness or bad behaviour in his hero, and his feelings within the relationship
are by far the stronger. Like Stanhope in *Journey's End*, Sassoon is the older man
and is much more experienced - not only as an officer, but also a poet. He
wants to guide Owen's poetry and assist him with its publication. Again,
though, there is no obvious symptom of romantic love displayed between Owen
and Sassoon, although in the novel, Sassoon is seen to doubt this, based on the
content and style of Owen's subsequent letters. The relationship between these
two poets is also explored in the play *Not About Heroes* by Stephen MacDonald,
told from Sassoon's perspective fourteen years after Owen's death.

Another male relationship which is explored in *Regeneration* is that between Billy
Prior and Dr Rivers. Like the relationship between Osborne and Stanhope, this is
more of a 'father-and-son' situation, but there any similarities end. Billy initially
resents Prior's interrogation of him and is abusive towards the doctor, until he
eventually realises that Rivers is the only person he can really trust. Rivers
understands Billy's troubled personality and wants to protect him even though
this must be done at a substantial personal cost to himself. Billy has managed to
penetrate Rivers' professional persona and, despite his concerns about this,
Rivers allows their strange relationship to continue. Pat Barker's use of this
relationship provides a good contrast within the novel with the friendship
between Sassoon and Dr Rivers, which is shown to be much deeper and more
considered.

A different perspective of a close male relationship can be seen in Susan Hill's
novel *Strange Meeting*. The two main characters in this story, Barton and Hilliard,
fall deeply in love. There is no evidence that their love is necessarily physical,
but that does not make it any less intense and meaningful - if anything the

opposite is the case. Although the reader is never made aware of the full nature of their relationship, it is, in fact, irrelevant to the story. Hilliard comes from a background devoid of affection and, finding this in Barton and his family, he is able, for the first time in his life, to experience love. There is not really an element of hero-worship between Barton and Hilliard, although the latter is slightly older and far more experienced. The portrayal of this relationship demonstrates the strength of love as an emotion: it can overcome everything - even the death of one of the parties involved and those touched by it can grow, gaining strength of character and understanding of others.

In *Regeneration* and *Strange Meeting*, the authors are free to be much more explicit about homosexual relationships. This was not a freedom which R C Sherriff would have been able to enjoy. It is unlikely that his play would have been performed had the content appeared homosexual. People at that time were still keen to ensure that the love that had existed between men during the war was "the right kind of love".

The poem *Comrades: An Episode* by Robert Nichols is a very good example of the love and respect which was often felt between officers and men in general, rather than a specific relationship between two men. It also demonstrates how this type of emotion came to have a greater significance, even than familial or romantic ties, due to the mens' shared experiences. Gates, the officer in this poem, lies wounded and dying in No-Man's-Land. Knowing that his life will shortly end, he decides that he must return to his men before he dies. This shows the admiration which he feels for them as well as his dependency on them - he literally decides that he *cannot* face death without seeing his men one last time. Two of his men are shot and killed trying to help him get back into the trench and by the end he bitterly regrets the cost of his decision to return. To the men, however, it would seem to have been an honour to give their lives for Gates. He was their officer and a man whom they held in the highest esteem. To read this poem helps the modern student understand the strength of emotion between men during the war, in a way that very few pieces achieve.

The way in which the war affects these relationships varies. In *Strange Meeting*, without the war, there may not have been a relationship in the first place. Barton and Hilliard come from very different backgrounds and meet for the first time at the front. In fact, the whole of their time together is spent there. They know that they might die at any moment and this serves to intensify their feelings for one another. The sense of impending loss and danger adds to the fear and risk necessarily involved in such a close friendship between two officers at this time.

In *Regeneration*, Sassoon and Owen also meet as a direct result of the war, but in completely different circumstances to Barton and Hilliard. There is not the same sense of fear involved in their relationship, partly due to the different nature of their friendship. Although Sassoon may, during his conversations with Dr Rivers, express some concerns over the consequences of an officer displaying homosexual tendencies, this did not necessarily apply to his feelings towards Owen. In the course of this novel, the effect of the war, other than to have placed them in Craiglockhart in the first place, is confined more to their future prospects and poetry as throughout most of the novel, we cannot be sure that either man will ever be passed fit to return to the active duty. Studying this relationship through the eyes of the play *Not About Heroes* could lead one to believe that both men felt a great deal more than is expressed in Pat Barker's novel. *Not About Heroes* takes their relationship on further in time, however, so we are able to see its development and the effect of Owen's death on his surviving friend.

In *Journey's End*, the circumstances of the main relationship are different again. Stanhope and Raleigh, had a pre-existing friendship so the entrance of the war into their lives has a profound effect on their relationship. Gone are the days of school cricket and rugby with Stanhope looking after his younger friend. Stanhope, who has been serving for many years, has become war-weary; his personality has changed, almost beyond recognition; his outlook has become tempered by his experiences. Sherriff shows us this disintegration of Stanhope's character through Raleigh's eyes, enabling us to experience his loss of innocence which occurs, in part, as he witnesses his friend's breakdown. Any trust which may have existed between these two before the war is now gone, as Stanhope realises he is no longer the same person that Raleigh used to worship. He cannot live up to Raleigh's high expectations and this only serves to heighten his sense of failure and make him more resentful of Raleigh's presence, as a reminder of the man he once was.

THE EFFECTS OF THE WAR ON THE INDIVIDUAL

The effects of the war on the individual is a popular topic for comparisons, and is represented in almost every form of literature within this genre. In *Journey's End*, the most obvious subject is Stanhope, whose personality has undergone a complete transformation. The audience only know him as the war-weary, cynical and embittered man of three year's war experience. Raleigh, on the other hand, knew him before he underwent these changes and this is how the audience gets to know of the effects of the war. The extent of the change in Stanhope's character is so great that neither man really seems to recognise the other when they first meet. This is a very simple device, employed by Sherriff, which enables the audience to understand how complete the transformation has been. Raleigh's character undergoes a change too, as he becomes more experienced. He really changes after he comes back from the raid which has cost Osborne's life. He cannot understand what has happened to him, and looks to Stanhope for reassurance, which he does not receive. This shows how, despite their former friendship, and Stanhope's generally protective nature, he is no longer able to help his friend - he is simply not capable anymore.

Sometimes authors portray the consequences of war in the form of a psychological trauma. This is the case in *The Return of the Soldier* by Rebecca West. Here, the hero, Chris Baldry has lost his memory and returned to his family home believing himself still to be twenty-one years old and in a relationship with his first-love, Margaret. His wife Kitty is, needless to say, shocked by his behaviour and the story is concerned with whether Chris should have treatment to bring him back to reality, or be allowed to remain in the, far happier, world he seems to now inhabit. The reader is not told exactly what has caused Chris's loss of memory, but it is clear from his changed appearance that his experiences of the war have taken their toll on him, both physically and emotionally. This novel not only outlines the effects of the war on the men who served in it, but also the consequences for their families and loved-ones back at home.

Another novel which shows this form of reaction to the war is *Regeneration* by Pat Barker. This story is set in a hospital for officers suffering from war neurosis, and centres mainly on the "curing" of various psychological problems relating to the mens' experiences in the war. Among these is Billy Prior, whose trauma is vividly described during a session of hypnosis. The novel sets out to explore the effects on these men, each of whom seems to have reacted in a different way. Billy Prior has become mute; Burns vomits whenever he is near food and Anderson has developed a morbid fear of the sight of blood, which is even more strange, given that he had been serving as a surgeon. The doctor in charge of these men, Dr W H R Rivers tries to get the men to talk about their experiences, and face their fears in order to lessen their importance. Although not always successful, this brings to light another aspect of the war's consequences as Dr Rivers himself becomes a victim of trauma. His conscience is constantly battling against his perceived duty. He knows that he must try to make the men better, but is also aware that in doing so, they may be sent back to the front and could be killed. Eventually he becomes so worn down by having to deal with the men in is care that he has a breakdown himself.

Not all authors use such obvious methods of demonstrating the effects of war on the individual. In many cases, it is not one single event which has the greatest impact, but a gradual wearing down of the nerves. One good example of this is *All Quiet on the Western Front*, in which Erich Maria Remarque shows how a young man, Paul Bäumer, sees all of his friends and comrades die or be badly wounded until eventually he gives up all hope for his own future. He believes that, if he survives, he may never be able to pick up the threads of his life before the war. This gradual breakdown which takes place during the novel shows how, eventually, everyone - even the most optimistic - reaches a point where they can simply not take any more.

By contrast, the main character in the novel *Birdsong*, Stephen Wraysford, is initially portrayed as comparatively unaffected by his experiences in the war. He is remote and cut-off from the events which are going on around him. This is due to his reaction to the end of his relationship with Isabelle Azaire, which has left him emotionally scarred. His self-imposed isolation ends with the death of his friend, Michael Weir and this episode marks a changing awareness in Stephen as he begins to realise his own capacity to care for his fellow man. Despite the appearance of being emotionally cut-off from his surroundings, the war obviously has an impact on Stephen as the reader later learns that after the war he did not speak for two years. This suggests that he had in fact been deeply affected by the various events he witnessed and he, presumably, felt the need to quietly assimilate and deal with his experiences, before he could begin to communicate again. Sebastian Faulks' intentions in the portrayal of Stephen Wraysford are arguably more complex. Stephen is shown to already have a troubled mind before the war, due to his childhood experiences and his broken relationship with Isabelle. He is portrayed as a man who has made the conscious decision to lock away his emotions and keep them in check, probably for fear of getting hurt again. No-one is allowed to get close to him. This portrayal helps the reader to understand that the effects of the war can be gradual, but are no less devastating than those of a man who experiences a single traumatic event.

The person who eventually pulls him back from this emotional void is Jeanne - Isabelle's sister - who helps him to rebuild his life and provides him with much needed stability.

Faulks also shows us how the war could have life-long consequences for those involved. The character of Brennan is seen as a confused and broken man, living in a world of his own in a Star and Garter Home. He has been existing like this for nearly sixty years - in other words since the end of the First World War.

THE EFFECTS OF DEATH AND LOSS ON THE INDIVIDUAL

The ways in which the characters deal with death is as varied as their own personalities and can differ greatly to their general reaction to the war, depending on the circumstances and on their relationship with the person who has died.

In *Journey's End*, Osborne's death is treated differently by the two main characters. Raleigh seems to feel guilty that he has survived while Osborne has died. This is partly because he has come to understand that Osborne was an essential character in Stanhope's life and he feels that he is somehow responsible for his loss. Also, he seems to be deeply affected by what he has witnessed during the raid, he becomes much quieter and more reserved than he had been previously and all of his enthusiasm has gone.

Stanhope, who has lost his best friend, reacts differently. To Raleigh, and the audience it *appears* that Stanhope does not care - he carries on as normal - even having a celebratory meal and joking around with the other officers. This dinner had been planned before the raid - Osborne and Raleigh had discussed it before they went out on their mission. However, during the dinner, there is an air of forced enjoyment as Stanhope tries to avoid discussing the raid or its consequences. To have cancelled the dinner would have been like admitting defeat - a trait not present in Stanhope's character - so the dinner must go ahead and Stanhope uses it as a means to drink and forget. This is because he knows that to think about Osborne's death will stop him functioning. He must continue to perform his duties because his men and the other officers are relying on him. In his nervous state, Stanhope understands that he cannot afford the luxury of grieving for his friend - he would be unable to cope if he actually did dwell on Osborne's death, and would probably fall apart completely.

When Raleigh dies, Stanhope is not given the opportunity to dwell on his schoolfriend's death as he is called upon to meet his own fate, although it is interesting to note that he gently touches Raleigh's head just before leaving the dugout, which seems to be an act of love and tenderness which we have not witnessed in Stanhope before.

Within this theme, one could also look at Raleigh's loss of Stanhope as his hero and friend. Raleigh appears shocked and disturbed by Stanhope's reaction to him and his frequent angry outbursts. Having grown up under Stanhope's protection, Raleigh must now face the destruction of his previously-held opinions. The change in both of these characters on Raleigh's death-bed and the momentary resumption of their old friendship allows Raleigh to die peacefully, with Stanhope heroic nature fully restored in his eyes.

In *Regeneration* Wilfred Owen has to face a different type of loss: he is so bewildered at the prospect of leaving Sassoon that he finds this sense of loss unquantifiable; many of the patients of Craiglockhart are there because they have been unable to cope, mentally, with the losses they have had to experience. Some of them have been permanently wounded, not physically, but psychologically and must learn to come to terms with this. As such, one of the main themes of *Regeneration* is this journey from initial loss to survival - the rebuilding of men.

Strange Meeting is probably one of the hopeful and uplifting pieces of First World War literature, yet the surviving character, Hilliard, has many personal losses to contend with. Not only has his beloved Barton been killed but his own leg has been amputated. Losing Barton has always been Hilliard's worst fear - he has always been unsure, having discovered love and his own capacity for it, that he could carry on living without the object of that love. His dependence on Barton has become paramount and due to this, he feels that the loss of his leg is of secondary importance. His own family hardly know how to react to him, but Barton's family pour out their affection and through this Hilliard is able to face the future. Susan Hill uses Hilliard's reaction to the the loss of Barton to demonstrate that a powerful and deep-rooted love, such as that which exists between these two characters, can overcome any obstacle and is far more long-lasting and ultimately satisfying than a quickly-spent passion.

There is a similar lesson to be learnt in *Birdsong* by Sebastian Faulks. Stephen Wraysford's passionate and illicit affair with Isabelle Azaire ends in his abandonment and forms the basis of his emotionally destroyed character. Throughout the novel, the reader is given the impression that Stephen cares little for his own life, and this remains so until he is faced with the prospect of losing it. During the tunnel scene where Stephen and Jack Firebrace are trapped underground, it is Stephen, rather than the religious Jack, who provides the hope for their future and encourages Jack to live for the sake of his wife. Once Jack is dead and Stephen is faced with his own mortality, he realises that the loss of Isabelle is less important to him than that he should be allowed to continue living. He understands also that Jeanne, Isabelle's sister, provides a hope for his future, and also he must live his life for the sake of all those who have died.

Erich Maria Remarque puts his central character, the young Paul Bäumer in *All Quiet on the Western Front*, through many harrowing experiences of loss. His friends - many of whom he was at school with - all die, until he is the only one left. For Paul, however, the most traumatic of these deaths is not one of his schoolfriends, but his comrade Stanislaus Katczinsky. Paul and Kat (as he is called) are together when Kat is injured. Paul carries his friend to a medical station where the orderly says they are too late - Kat is dead. At this moment Paul feels as if his life has ended: he can no longer feel anything but merely exists from that point onwards. Effectively, his life ceases with the loss of his friend.

Several poets wrote movingly of their grief and facing the future after so many deaths. Edith Nesbit, for example, in *The Fields of Flanders* writes of the debt of gratitude she feels for the sacrifices being demanded of, and made by so many young men. This is a debt which, in her view, can never be repaid. This sentiment is echoed in Wilfrid Wilson Gibson's *Lament* which beautifully evokes his sense of loss. Gibson is asking here how he is supposed to carry on living knowing that so many have given up everything to gain his freedom. This sense of gratitude, mixed with grief and even an element of guilt results in everything he does and sees being tinged with heartbreak - a feeling which he realises he will have to live with for the rest of his life. To Gibson, the pain of such a life is worse than death itself.

Some poets addressed poems to specific people who had died. For example Vera Brittain's poem *Perhaps* is addressed to her fiancé Roland Leighton who died on 23rd December 1915. In this poem she recites, with great sadness, all of the things she will no longer enjoy or will never be able to do, because he is not with her. Siegfried Sassoon's poem *To Any Dead Officer* was originally addressed to Lieutenant E. L. Orme who was killed in action on 27th May 1917. Here, Sassoon reminisces about happier times, when they had laughed together, before going on to describe his friend's death and how pointless it seems. Although, in typical Sassoon style, the poem ends on a note of irony, his emotions are very much on the surface in this piece and his acute sense of loss, which is thinly masked by humour, is profoundly moving. The sense that some were unable to ever forget their war experiences and the losses they suffered, is brought to life in Edmund Blunden's poem *1916 seen from 1921*. Here he describes a tremendous feeling of loss and sadness. The reader becomes acutely aware that he is biding his time, waiting for his life to return to him, so that he can once again be at peace in his beloved countryside, but one also realises that he never really achieved this aim. Like so many others, he was never truly able to forget.

RESPONSIBILITY

Another aspect of the war, which is worthy of examination is that of responsibility - looking after the men. In *Journey's End* it is clear throughout that Stanhope always puts his men first. He regards himself as their father-figure, although in many cases he is much younger than them. He knows and accepts that it is his responsibility to ensure that his men are at their best, both for their own benefit and for the good of the company as a whole.

Pat Barker gives Sassoon's reason for wanting to return to the front in *Regeneration*, as his desire to be back with his men and to be of service to them. He has a strong sense of guilt that he is safe, whilst they are dying in France. Robert Graves points out that this feeling was mutual and, in reality,   In reality, Sassoon wrote his poem *Banishment* at this time which portrays his feelings for the men he had left behind, and his desire to right any wrongs he may have done them.

In *Strange Meeting* David Barton, like Stanhope, is quite prepared to discuss his own fears in order to ease those of his men. However, Hilliard's main concern is the welfare of Barton. That is not to say that he doesn't care about the other men in his company, but he knows that, due to his own emotional inadequacies, Barton is better suited and more able to meet their needs. He feels that, for everybody's sake, but especially his own, Barton must be kept safe, and this becomes the main focus of his attention throughout the novel.

These portrayals are quite realistic and the officer commanding a company of men was often expected to be a mother-figure, as well as a father-figure, to his men. It was his responsibility to ensure that the men were fed, washed, had somewhere to sleep, kept their equipment clean etc. In addition, he also had to provide moral support to the men and listen to their problems, trying to help solve them if possible. Given the extreme youth of most of these officers, like Stanhope, it is hardly surprising that they occasionally buckled under the weight of so many demands.

One poet who typified this attitude was E. A. Mackintosh whose love and feelings of responsibility for his men is the main theme of much of his poetry. *In Memoriam* is a particularly good example of this and demonstrates how much like a father-figure he felt, as well as his sense of pride at being the officer in charge of his men, for whom he had a great respect and admiration. The story behind this moving poem is interesting. During a raid, one of Mackintosh's men, Private David Sutherland, was wounded. Mackintosh carried him for some time until it became clear that the young soldier was dead and Mackintosh was forced to leave his body behind in order to help others get back to their trenches. He actually managed to bring in two other men under heavy fire and was awarded the Military Cross for his courage. Despite this, he was overwhelmed by guilt for having left Sutherland's body in No Man's Land and this poem demonstrates his feelings of inadequacy for having, in his own mind, 'failed' this young man.

A QUESTION OF COMPARISONS

Many students have to make direct comparisons between two particular texts, demonstrating the author's treatment of a specific topic. Where this is dealt with as coursework, some examination boards allow that the student may be permitted to choose the texts for themselves. To that end, we have included a list of possible topics and suggested texts which, in our opinion, provide suitable material for such essays, assuming that *Journey's End* will be one of the texts involved.

THE EFFECTS OF THE WAR ON THE INDIVIDUAL

This can take the form of a psychological or emotional response either to the war in general or to a specific event. Students are expected to show an understanding of an author's treatment of this subject.

Using Journey's End and Regeneration

Good examples of this subject matter can be found in Stanhope's character in *Journey's End* and in Billy Prior in *Regeneration* by Pat Barker. Sherriff shows us the disintegration of Stanhope through the eyes of his schoolfriend Raleigh and makes it clear that his problems stem from the length of service he has seen. Billy Prior, on the other hand, has become traumatised by a solitary experience, although during his treatment it becomes clear that his psychological problems are the result of a build-up of distressing happenings.

Stanhope and Prior have different backgrounds and both authors use these backgrounds to demonstrate their characters and show us that their upbringing and education form an integral part of their reactions and behaviour during the war. Students should therefore look at the descriptions of their characters before the war and contrast these with their personalities during the conflict in order to assess the impact of their experiences.

Using Journey's End and Strange Meeting

Raleigh's initial experience of the war during the raid changes him from a young naive adventurer into a shocked and disturbed young man. In Strange Meeting, the character of David Barton undergoes a similar transformation. David Barton is a pleasant, keen and innocent new recruit, who changes following a harrowing spell in the front line trenches.

Susan Hill portrays Barton's reactions in the form of his silence and withdrawal, which contrasts with his previously outgoing character. His close friend Hilliard tries to draw out a response from Barton, and there is a role reversal here, as the formerly quiet, reticent Hilliard helps Barton to adjust to what has happened. Raleigh, on the other hand, is clearly keen to discuss his experiences with Stanhope, who is incapable of assisting him.

In this instance, there are several characters and reactions to examine: Stanhope and Hilliard, who have not directly experienced these traumatic events themselves react differently to their friends' requirements. Barton and Raleigh are both traumatised by what they have seen, but they respond differently. Students should look at the relationships portrayed between the individuals and assess their influence on the outcome.

THE PRESENTATION OF HEROISM

Students can take several different views of this subject, from hero-worship, to a man's perception of heroism or courage - whether his own, or that of someone else.

Using Journey's End and Regeneration

When looking at hero worship, an excellent example can be found in the feelings of Raleigh for Stanhope. This emotion forms the basis of their relationship and students should also pay attention to Stanhope's reaction to Raleigh's arrival. Stanhope, it would seem, had taken his heroic status quite seriously while at school and feels under extreme pressure to continue with this at the front.

In *Regeneration*, Pat Barker has used the real-life relationship between Siegfried Sassoon and Wilfred Owen to show how strong the feeling of hero-worship can be. Owen is in awe of his older friend and, when the two part, his loss is almost incalculable.

Using these two books to demonstrate heroism, or the perception of heroism, is equally viable. In *Journey's End*, many of the characters are given heroic traits. Osborne, for example, faces the raid with an outward calm which is quite remarkable. He is an experienced officer who has undertaken such tasks in the past, and yet he approaches this mission with an inspiring level-headedness. Stanhope's understanding of courage and heroism is also worth noting here. He feels he has failed, and in turning to alcohol for courage, he feels disappointed that his nerves have let him down. However, throughout the play, we are shown that this is not the case. Although his three years of traumatic service have taken their toll, he never lacks courage and always puts the wellbeing and safety of others before himself.

Most of the characters in *Regeneration*, are in Craiglockhart hospital because of either a mental or physical breakdown and many of them display true courage in facing up to their fears and trying to return to a normal life. Billy Prior's perception of his own trauma is to not believe that something so 'insignificant' could have caused him to breakdown. Like Stanhope, he believes that his nerves have failed him and appears disappointed in his own courage. Rivers must help him to rebuild his self-confidence and face the future.

Using Journey's End and Birdsong

When comparing these two pieces, the nature of the heroism involved is more that of rising above one's circumstances. For example, the character of Trotter in *Journey's End* seems to not show any fear or feelings at all for the situation in which he has found himself. This demonstrates a true courage: to appear to carry on almost as normal despite his circumstances, which shows us the true nature of Trotter's character - the down to earth soldier, who simply gets on with the job at hand. Sherriff's use of Trotter to this end, forces the audience to realise that heroism is not all about dashing around 'appearing' brave, but has much more to do with facing fear every day, and carrying on regardless.

In *Birdsong*, the central character, Stephen Wraysford also seems to keep going, regardless. In this instance, however, Sebastian Faulks is using this to demonstrate Wraysford's numbness - he simply does not feel anything due to his emotional torment following Isabelle's abandonment of him. Isabelle herself shows an element of bravery when she falls in love with a German soldier, knowing that this will necessitate her rejection by everyone she holds dear. She knowingly abandons her life in France to be with Max, realising that she will never be able to return again.

In addition, Sebastian Faulks shows us a character who manages to overcome a terrible personal loss and yet continue with his duties. Jack Firebrace, the tunneller, loses his son, but still manages to keep going and perform the tasks he is set. Eventually Jack does succumb to death, but only after he has faced the very worst that life has to throw at him, and to rise above it.

Students who approach this topic should bear in mind that 'heroism' or 'courage' had very different meanings before and during the First World War to a modern-day perception, when we are apt to give famous footballers or screen idols a heroic status. The characters in these pieces must face their own fears or their own potential deaths, in the full knowledge of the consequences.

THE EFFECTS OF THE WAR ON MALE RELATIONSHIPS

Within this topic, students can choose whether to focus on relationships which pre-existed the war, or those which have been formed during, and because of, the conflict.

Using Journey's End and All Quiet on the Western Front

In both of these cases, the authors use both types of male relationship mentioned above. In *Journey's End*, Raleigh and Stanhope had known each other before the war, but Stanhope's greatest friendship is with Osborne, a man much older and wiser than himself, upon whom he has come to depend. Stanhope's friendship with Raleigh is, of necessity, completely different to the one they shared at school, which Raleigh finds difficult to accept.

A similar situation occurs in *All Quiet on the Western Front*. Here Paul Bäumer is serving at the front with many of his schoolfriends, but his greatest ally is a man twice his age, whom he only met once he had enlisted: Stanislaus Katczinsky. One by one, Paul's friends are killed, or seriously injured, but it is Kat's death which has the greatest impact on him. He literally cannot see the point in going on any longer.

Stanhope's reaction to Osborne's death is different: although he is naturally deeply affected, he cannot simply stop. As an officer, too many other people are relying on him for him to allow himself the luxury of grieving. Herein lies one of he fundamental contrasts between these two books and how the authors deal with emotional elements. The characters in *Journey's End* are all officers, mainly from the upper classes, and therefore to openly show emotions would not have been acceptable behaviour. In *All Quiet on the Western Front*, however, the central characters are all ranking soldiers, whose emotions are allowed to the surface. Remarque's story is told through the eyes of Paul Bäumer, who forms an attachment to a 'father-figure'. Sherriff, on the other hand, whilst acknowledging Stanhope's need for Osborne, never allows the audience to forget who is the most senior officer.

Using Journey's End and Strange Meeting

These two works contain different types of relationship, and both of them show how the war can impact greatly. In *Journey's End*, the relationship between Raleigh and Stanhope is adversely affected by Raleigh's arrival in Stanhope's Company. Until that point, Raleigh had only been a memory of schooldays for Stanhope, as well as being the brother of Madge and both of these were things he had chosen not to think about too much. Raleigh's arrival serves to remind Stanhope of everything that he has lost. The war's impact on this relationship is to almost fracture it completely. Stanhope cannot accept Raleigh's presence until the very end when Raleigh is dying. It is only at this point that Stanhope can lower his guard and allow his former personality to come through to the aid of his young friend.

Conversely, in *Strange Meeting*, the relationship between Barton and Hilliard only starts as a direct result of the war. These two characters had no previous knowledge of one another and come from very different family backgrounds. The fact that they fall in love during the war shows that not all of the effects of the conflict are negative. In fact, Susan Hill's portrayal of this relationship is probably one of the more hopeful and deeply affecting pieces of First World War literature. The reader is left with the overriding impression that love can conquer absolutely everything - even death.

One of the main reasons behind the differences in these two pieces could be the time at which they were written. *Journey's End* was first performed in 1928 while *Strange Meeting* was published in 1971. As stated earlier in this guide, this time difference allowed Susan Hill a far greater freedom to hint at a homosexual relationship between her main characters than would have been afforded to R C Sherriff. However, Susan Hill does not choose to openly mention homosexuality. She leaves this to the reader's imagination and prefers instead to portray a close, loving and intense relationship which has been brought about because of the war, rather than being ruined by it.

CITY AND ISLINGTON
SIXTH FORM COLLEGE
283-309 GOSWELL ROAD
LONDON EC1V 7LA
TEL 020 7520 0652

Contemporary Reviews

When *Journey's End* was first performed at the Apollo Theatre on the 9th and 10th of December 1928, the critics arrived to watch the production on the second showing and Sherriff waited anxiously on the morning of the 11th to discover their opinion. He need not have feared: the play was well received.

Hannan Swaffer - a much feared critic, writing for the *Daily Express*, began his piece with the headline: "The greatest of all war plays", continuing:

"A new dramatist, R. C. Sherriff, achieved the distinction of compelling to real emotion an audience who were watching a play almost without plot, with no women in the cast!... It was a remarkable achievement... Journey's End is perhaps the greatest of all war plays... This is the English theatre at its best... There is no shirking the facts: no concession to fashion... It is perfectly acted; each actor cuts a little cameo of stark reality... All London should flock to see it. It carries a great lesson - one that is nobly told..."

Later that evening, James Agate, critic for *The Times* gave his weekly theatre review on the radio. In this he usually spoke of three or four productions, but on that evening he dedicated his entire programme to *Journey's End*, saying:

"I've just seen a play called Journey's End, and I shall talk of nothing else tonight but of this fine piece of work. I have never been so deeply moved, so enthralled, so exalted... Lest you think it a sombre unrelieved tragedy I must tell you of a cook-batman whose every appearance brought the house down."

After the production went on at The Savoy Theatre on 21st January 1929, Sherriff again wondered whether the critics would be kind and, again, his fears were unfounded. The headlines spoke for themselves:

"This noble war play" - the *Morning Post*

"Great War Drama" - the *Daily Mail*

"Fine New War Play" - the *Mirror*

"No one should miss seeing this play" - the *Daily News*

The reviews themselves were even more fulsome:

"Everyone must see Journey's End... It could and should be translated into the language of every ex-ally and ex-enemy" said the critic in the *Chronicle*.

"Once inside the theatre, no one will be other than enthralled," was the comment in the *Daily Sketch*.

"Mr R. C. Sherriff's war play Journey's End, made a profound impression when it was given a trial production by the Stage Society in December, and now that it has been put on for a run at the Savoy Theatre we may look to it to make an impression equally profound upon a wider public... The author has achieved that rare feat of bringing to complete accomplishment what he set out to do... not for a long time has any serious play been so rapturously received." is how the play was reported in the *Telegraph*.

When the play opened on Broadway, the American critics were equally enthusiastic, writing headlines such as:

"The finest play to reach Broadway in years" and "The best ambassador sent to America by Britain".

Having starred in the first two performances at the Apollo Theatre, Laurence Olivier was unable to continue with the remaining cast when the play was put on at the Savoy Theatre, as he had been given the lead role in Beau Geste at His Majesty's Theatre. Everyone was disappointed about losing their leading man, but Sherriff was gratified in later years to read a biography of Olivier in which he stated that his favourite theatre role had been playing Stanhope in Journey's End. Given the roles that Olivier must have performed, and that he only played the part for two shows, this is high praise indeed.

Sherriff himself put the success of the play down to its realism: he hadn't set out to preach a message about war and its rights or wrongs, but to portray it as it really was. This allowed former soldiers, war widows and anyone who had any understanding of the conflict to relate to and learn from it.

FURTHER READING RECOMMENDATIONS FOR A-LEVEL STUDENTS

Students of A-Level standard are expected to demonstrate a sound knowledge of the texts they are studying and also to enhance this knowledge with extensive reading of other texts within the subject. We have provided on the following pages a list of books, poetry, plays and non-fiction which, in our opinion, provide a good basic understanding of this topic.

Plays and Drama
As well as *Journey's End*, students could also read any of the following:

The Accrington Pals by Peter Whelan
This play follows a group of men who have volunteered to join their local Pals battalion. Written from the perspective of those who are left behind, we are shown the impact on their everyday lives when almost all of the men have gone away to fight. The realistic tragedy of this play is that when the Pals participated in the Battle of the Somme towns, such as Accrington, suffered great losses which would affect almost every inhabitant.

Oh! What a Lovely War by Joan Littlewood
A satire about the First World War told using newsreels, documents and songs. First performed in 1963, this is as much a play about the 1960's as about the First World War and promotes the 'Lions led by Donkeys' theory which was prevalent at that time.

Not About Heroes by Stephen MacDonald
Probably one of the most underrated First World War plays, this details the friendship between Wilfred Owen and Siegfried Sassoon, from their initial meeting at Craiglockhart, to Owen's death. Told from Sassoon's perspective, it is a humourous, tragic and above all, moving account of this friendship and is based on diary entries and extracts from letters and autobiographies.

In addition, students of *Journey's End* could also watch *Blackadder Goes Forth* starring Rowan Atkinson paying particular attention to the final episode. Although this screenplay was written in the late 20th century, much of the atmosphere and 'gallows' humour could prove useful in understanding this play, especially when students are unable to see a live performance.

Novels

Strange Meeting by Susan Hill
Strange Meeting is a beautiful and moving book. It is the story of two young men, who meet in the worst circumstances, yet manage to overcome their surroundings and form a deep and lasting friendship. Susan Hill writes so evocatively that the reader is automatically drawn into the lives of these men: the sights, sounds and even smells which they witness are brought to life. It is a book about war and its effects; it is also a story of love, both conventional and 'forbidden'; of human relationships of every variety. This is a tale told during the worst of times, about the best of men.

Birdsong by Sebastian Faulks
This novel tells the story of Stephen Wraysford, his destructive pre-war love-affair, his war experiences and, through the eyes of his grand-daughter, the effects of the war on his personality and his generation. A central theme to this story is man's ability to overcome adversity: to rise above his circumstances and survive - no matter what is thrown in his path.

A Long Long Way by Sebastian Barry
This is a story about Willie Dunne, a young Irish volunteer serving in the trenches of the Western Front. Willie must not only contend with the horrors of the war, but also his own confused feelings regarding the Easter uprising of 1916, and his father's disapproval. This novel is about loyalty, betrayal, fear, wisdom, discovery and, above all, love.

A Very Long Engagement by Sebastien Japrisot
This is a story of enduring love and determination. Refusing to believe that her lover can possibly have left her forever, Mathilde decides to search for Manech whom she has been told is missing, presumed dead. She learns from a first-hand witness, that he may not have died, so she sets out on a voyage of discovery - learning not just about his fate, but also a great deal about herself and human nature.

Regeneration by Pat Barker
This book is, as its title implies, a novel about the rebuilding of men following extreme trauma. *Regeneration* is a story of man's exploration of his inner being - his mind, feelings and reactions. It details the effects of war on a generation of young men who, because of their experiences, would no longer be able to live ordinary lives.

The Return of the Soldier by Rebecca West
Written in 1918, this home-front novel gives a useful insight into the trauma of war, as seen through the eyes of three women. Chris Baldry, an officer and husband of Kitty, returns home suffering from shell-shock and amnesia, believing that he is still in a relationship with Margaret Allington - his first love. Kitty, Margaret and Chris's cousin, Jenny, must decide whether to leave Chris in his make-believe world, safe from the war; or whether to 'cure' him and risk his future welfare once he returns to being a soldier.

All Quiet on the Western Front by Erich Maria Remarque
Written from first-hand experience of life in the trenches, this novel is the moving account of the lives of a group of young German soldiers during the First World War. The fact that this, often shocking, story is told from a German perspective demonstrates the universal horrors of the war and the sympathy between men of both sides for others enduring the same hardships as themselves.

Poetry

It is recommended that students read from a wide variety of poets, including female writers. The following anthologies provide good resources for students.

Poems of the First World War - Never such Innocence
Edited by Martin Stephen
Probably one of the most comprehensive and accessible anthologies of First World War poetry. The notes which accompany each chapter are not over-long or too complicated and leave the poetry to speak for itself.

Lads: Love Poetry of the Trenches by Martin Taylor
Featuring many lesser-known poets and poems, this anthology approaches the First World War from a different perspective: love. A valuable introduction discusses the emotions of men who, perhaps for the first time, were discovering their own capacity to love their fellow man. This is not an anthology of purely homo-erotic poems, but also features verses by those who had found affection and deep lasting friendship in the trenches of the First World War.

Scars Upon My Heart, Selected by Catherine Reilly
A collection of poems written exclusively by women on the subject of the First World War. Some of the better known female poets are featured here, together with the more obscure, and authors who are not now renowned for their poetry, but for their works in other areas of literature.

Non-Fiction

Undertones of War by Edmund Blunden
Edmund Blunden's memoir of his experiences in the First World War is a moving and enlightening book, demonstrating above all the intense feelings of respect and comradeship which Blunden found in the trenches.

Memoirs of an Infantry Officer by Siegfried Sassoon
Following on from *Memoirs of a Fox-hunting Man*, this book is an autobiographical account of Sassoon's life during the First World War. Sassoon has changed the names of the characters and George Sherston (Sassoon) is not a poet. Sassoon became one of the war's most famous poets and this prose account of his war provides useful background information.
(For a list of the fictional characters and their factual counterparts, see Appendix II of *Siegfried Sassoon by John Stuart Roberts*.)

1914-1918: Voices and Images of the Great War by Lyn MacDonald
One of the most useful 'unofficial' history books available to those studying the First World War. This book tells the story of the soldiers who fought the war through their letters, diary extracts, newspaper reports, poetry and eye-witness accounts.

Letters from a Lost Generation (First World War Letters of Vera Brittain and Four Friends)
Edited by Alan Bishop and Mark Bostridge
A remarkable insight into the changes which the First World War caused to a particular set of individuals. In this instance, Vera Brittain lost four important people in her life (two close friends, her fiancé and her brother). The agony this evoked is demonstrated through letters sent between these five characters, which went on to form the basis of Vera Brittain's autobiography *Testament of Youth*.

The Western Front by Richard Holmes
This is one of many history books about the First World War. Dealing specifically with the Western Front, Richard Holmes looks at the creation of the trench warfare system, supplying men and munitions, major battles and living on the front line.

To the Last Man: Spring 1918 by Lyn MacDonald
This is an invaluable book for anyone studying *Journey's End* as it helps in the understanding of the personalities involved and the time through which they were living. As with all of Lyn MacDonald's excellent books, *To the Last Man* tells its story through the words of the people who were there. It is not restricted to a British perspective, but tells of the first few months of 1918 and their momentous consequences from every angle. The author gives just the right amount of background information of a political and historical nature to keep the reader interested and informed, while leaving the centre-stage to those who really matter... the men themselves.

BIBLIOGRAPHY

The First World War
by John Keegan

Chronology of the Great War, 1914-1918
Edited by Lord Edward Gleichen

To the Last Man: Spring 1918
by Lyn MacDonald

Rosebriars Trust
rosebriars.org.uk

Journey's End
by R C Sherriff

Strange Meeting
by Susan Hill

The Return of the Soldier
by Rebecca West

All Quiet on the Western Front
by Erich Maria Remarque

Scars Upon My Heart
Edited by Catherine Reilly

Never Such Innocence
Edited by Martin Stephen

The British Expeditionary Force 1914-15
Bruce Gudmundsson

No Leading Lady: An Autobiography
by R C Sherriff

The Private War Letters of R C Sherriff

OTHER TITLES

GWLSRC PRINTABLE ONLINE RESOURCE PACKAGES:

A Long Long Way
All Quiet on the Western Front
Birdsong
Edward Thomas Collection
Journey's End (A-Level or GCSE)
Not About Heroes
Not So Quiet...
OCR Opening Lines Section F
OCR Opening Lines Section H
Oh What a Lovely War
Oxford Book of War Poetry Anthology
Regeneration
Scars Upon My Heart Anthology
Siegfried Sassoon Collection
Strange Meeting (Susan Hill)
The Accrington Pals
The Eye in the Door
The First Casualty
The Ghost Road
The Return of the Soldier
Wilfred Owen Collection
Up The Line to Death Anthology

GREAT WAR LITERATURE TEACHER RESOURCES:

Wilfred Owen: OCR AS F661
Wilfred Owen: OCR GCSE A661
Edward Thomas: OCR AS F661
Regeneration
Birdsong

GREAT WAR LITERATURE STUDY GUIDE E-BOOKS:

NOVELS & PLAYS

All Quiet on the Western Front
Birdsong
Journey's End (A-Level or GCSE)
Regeneration
The Eye in the Door
The Ghost Road
A Long Long Way
The First Casualty
Strange Meeting
The Return of the Soldier
The Accrington Pals
Not About Heroes
Oh What a Lovely War

POET BIOGRAPHIES AND POETRY ANALYSIS:

Herbert Asquith
Harold Begbie
John Peale Bishop
Edmund Blunden
Vera Brittain
Rupert Brooke
Thomas Burke
May Wedderburn Cannan
Margaret Postgate Cole
Alice Corbin
E E Cummings
Nancy Cunard
T S Eliot
Eleanor Farjeon
Gilbert Frankau
Robert Frost
Wilfrid Wilson Gibson
Anna Gordon Keown
Robert Graves

Julian Grenfell
Ivor Gurney
Thomas Hardy
Alan P Herbert
Agnes Grozier Herbertson
W N Hodgson
A E Housman
Geoffrey Anketell Studdert Kennedy
Winifred M Letts
Amy Lowell
E A Mackintosh
John McCrae
Charlotte Mew
Edna St Vincent Millay
Ruth Comfort Mitchell
Harriet Monroe
Edith Nesbit
Robert Nichols
Wilfred Owen
Jessie Pope
Ezra Pound
Florence Ripley Mastin
Isaac Rosenberg
Carl Sandburg
Siegfried Sassoon
Alan Seeger
Charles Hamilton Sorley
Wallace Stevens
Sara Teasdale
Edward Wyndham Tennant
Lesbia Thanet
Edward Thomas
Iris Tree
Katharine Tynan Hinkson
Robert Ernest Vernède
Arthur Graeme West

Please note that e-books are only available direct from our Web site at
www.greatwarliterature.co.uk and cannot be purchased through bookshops.

NOTES

NOTES

NOTES

Printed in Great Britain
by Amazon.co.uk, Ltd.,
Marston Gate.